THE URGENCY OF AWARENESS

Unlocking the Power within Individual, Organizational, and Community Efforts

Authored by

Jodi R. Pfarr

with Illustrating Life Stories by

Allison Boisvert

MCP BOOKS

MCP Books
2301 Lucien Way #415
Maitland, FL 32751
407.339.4217
www.millcitypress.net

Development editing by Rebecca Ninke
Book design by Erisha L. Menon

Printed in the United States of America

Paperback ISBN-13: 978-1-6350-5290-9
eBook ISBN-13: 978-1-6305-0357-4

LCCN: 2019920050

THE
URGENCY
OF
AWARENESS

This book is dedicated to
Trina, John, Jerri, and all those
who give of themselves so others may have…
Marian, with love
and
In loving memory of Allison Boisvert.

TABLE OF CONTENTS

INTRODUCTION BY THE AUTHOR AND ALLISON BOISVERT

ALLISON BOISVERT

I grew up living in poverty, in both Native American and European American cultures. In and out of social service institutions, my eventual success in supporting myself and my family was learned through mentors, including social workers who helped me become more aware of how the world worked, how my experiences impacted me, and the existence of tools of stability. My life work in the social service field was inspired by these role models—people who had high expectations of me, who gave me respectful guidance, who heard me, and who took time to teach me about the world I lived in. This awareness increased my efforts to be successful in the world.

Having learned about social services from the inside out, I often observed efforts in my field differently than my colleagues. I was no-nonsense, seeking only practical and effective solutions. "Feel good" work that had little positive impact was dismissed. I loved my career working with those who were generationally impoverished, and I remain deeply interested in understanding why some make it out but many do not.

After thirty-five years of work, I retired with a plan to live happily ever after in my cabin in the woods with my dogs, cable TV, and a library card. That plan lasted two months. Retirement was a myth to which I could not relate. What did retirement mean? Now how do I matter?

I came back to the city and found a job as a justice minister for a large Catholic community. It was familiar territory and my best job ever. I loved it, but fate had other plans.

There was need for a biopsy. The next day, three young, grim-faced doctors visited me. After a few introductions and pleasantries, I began to hear phrases like "pancreatic cancer," "terminal," and "time may be extended with surgery and chemo." I could only think, What? Who me?

When I first received a terminal cancer diagnosis, I was consumed with fear, panic, and profound grief. It was hell. Then I started to figure out how to cope. I bumbled around until the day my sister told me not to let the cancer define me. Before the diagnosis, I had decided that my personal goal was to become a better person, a more authentic communicator, and a bridge-builder of relationships. Now it was time to get on the stick. No longer burdened with the ego of youth, I was liberated from the constraints of so many things I had once thought so very important. Even (or especially) with a terminal diagnosis, I was free to work on my personal goal and expand the gifts I had been given.

My growth was dependent on becoming acutely aware of my thoughts about people, places, and things. How to start? How to move beyond fear and anxiety? Somewhere along the line, I had been told anxiety lies in the gap between the past and the future. We never know the future, but we have this moment, so my answer was to simply live in the moment.

When people are able to speak honestly about my current reality, they often ask me what I have learned and what now really matters. In my new freedom, these have become my priorities:

Presence: You've heard it before in different ways—be in the moment, stay engaged, be present, be here and now. What do those things really mean? Reflecting on meaningful moments in my life, I realized that the most significant times were those when I felt heard. Someone was really there with me; I was listened to without distraction. The person I was with was in that moment, not thinking about the argument she had with her spouse the night before or thinking about what he was going to have for dinner.

On the other hand, I recognize that most mistakes I've made were due to not quieting my internal monologue, not paying attention, and not being fully present.

I just read Success through Stillness (Simmons, 2014), a book co-authored by hip-hop mogul Russell Simmons. He writes,
> "I can honestly say that without that stillness, there's no way I'd be where I am today. Not only professionally, but personally and spiritually too." (Simmons and Morrow, 2014, p.15.)

And,

> "I was able to slow down and see that my success had always been in those moments of stillness that I'd experienced. And that the more I could access that stillness, then the more happiness and success I could experience." (Simmons and Morrow, 2014, p.14.)

Practice: *How do we stay in the present? Practice, practice, practice. Anything that is good for us requires a decision, then the work in making it happen begins.*

Becoming present has to be intentional. I work on staying present by meditating several times a day. Some use prayer in the same way to clear the mind, quiet the fierce ego battles going on, and pay attention to breathing. Checking in with myself about every hour, I ask myself, are you truly present or stuck in the past or future? If a thought pops up—and it does constantly—I just let it go and refocus my breath. The more I meditate, the easier it becomes. However, it does require discipline as it is so easy to respond to the constant stimulation of our culture that keeps chaos alive. The spiritual mentor Ram Dass teaches that society values information, not wisdom. We need more wisdom in our own lives and in the world. I believe that wisdom is only gained through quiet self-reflection.

Benevolent Detachment: *Being still and staying in the present is really difficult; the ego is always fighting for attention. However, it is well worth the effort. One of the benefits is learning to detach with benevolence. You can look closely at situations and relationships, compassionately seeing them for what they are, without unnecessary drama. You are better able to manage your own life and emotions when you realize you do not control the outcomes for others. You can remove unhelpful pain, guilt, and grief, as well as inappropriate engagement.*

We all have a natural tendency to become entangled in the chaos and drama of life. I believe poverty exacerbates this tendency. Responding to chaos and drama can give a false sense of control and power; it feeds the ego that pretends to know how things should be.

Let me give you an example from my life. My second son suffers from profound alcoholism and drug addiction. There have been multiple treatments and many forms of maternal assistance including living at home, lending money, cosigning for car loans, etc. I tried to make things better, but nothing worked. I was stuck in a heavy state of tension, fear, despair, anger, and terrible guilt.

Then I realized that I had to let go. I had to learn to forgive myself. I had to accept that I cannot cure him. I recognized that this was his journey, not mine. Jumping on board with the chaos and drama of his lifestyle was not helpful to either of us. I needed to cultivate a benevolent detachment. I still long for my son, but I do not engage in the drama of the day. I fully realize that this is his journey and with all the love in my heart and soul, I commend him to the universe. The outcome of his life is not something I can control. If change is to occur, it will be because of his own enlightened efforts.

I wanted to share in a lasting way what wisdom I have gained living a diverse and eventful life. Jodi Pfarr created a highly effective and engaging day-long workshop that invites participants into an awareness of how living in a societal system that labels us can limit our potential, both personally and professionally. I knew my life stories and wisdom, gleaned through experience, would align beautifully with the lessons she was teaching, so I asked Jodi to use my stories to illustrate her work. And thus, the creation of this book emerged.

I am very aware that by the time this book is published, I will have crossed over. My docs say I am already a miracle, having lived over three years with a pancreatic cancer diagnosis. I hope you find this work helpful on your journey.

Allison Boisvert passed away on June 26, 2015, at the age of seventy-two.

JODI R. PFARR

My relationship with Allison began when she was my boss's boss. She was one of a few bosses who emanated self-awareness and openness to others' insight and experience. Every time we met, I felt listened to, like someone understood me, yet challenged me to be more. Over the years, she became my elder and finally my Whe heh — one who guides me on my path. When asked if her life story could be used to support the training and concepts I had created for my work, she agreed. I was deeply humbled and honored. I had shaped a training that invites people to have a deeper awareness of our diverse world: how it impacts us, our institutions, and our communities, and how to unlock potential. Allison's motto of "Presence, Practice, and Benevolent Detachment" was the ultimate embodiment of this. Once we decided to create a book together, we met regularly to merge Allison's powerful illustrations with my concepts. Because chemotherapy had damaged her eyes, it was difficult for her to read and write, so I videoed Allison telling her story and offering deeper understanding to her motto. Some of these videos can be viewed online at www.jpfarr.com.

Allison was a remarkable woman with profound insight. Since her death in June 2015, she is deeply missed, though you only have to feel the wind blow off the lake on your face on a cool Minnesota night to know she is still with us. It is my hope that you find our book helpful for more effectively navigating your personal and professional lives.

—Jodi

BEFORE YOU BEGIN...

This book invites you into a new awareness of your experience and then challenges you to analyze how your experience affects how you function and interact. You will learn about others' experiences and ultimately gain new keys that can increase effective communication and improve outcomes. Allison's narrative voice will illustrate my concepts in an easily grasped manner; we have changed the font to indicate what is in her voice.

The material in this book is most effective for group study, ideally with five to ten participants who hold as many different experiences (ages, genders, skin color, economic classes) from each other as possible. Hearing about other people's experiences while processing chapter discussion questions and exercises will greatly enrich the understanding of the material. Suggestions for facilitators are located in the back of the book. Individuals also can benefit from reading the material on their own, writing out answers to the discussion questions, and completing the exercises.

There is an urgency of awareness in our world. The time you spend on this topic is appreciated and will help you unlock the power of awareness in both personal and professional settings. Thank you for your commitment to learning in our increasingly diverse world.

The goal of this book is to apply the themes of presence, practice, and benevolent detachment to our societal system so that we may unlock the power to living and working well within it.

Presence: The first two chapters of this book invite us to become aware of our experience within a societal system that intrinsically categorizes us. We are challenged to grow in our understanding of how the labels of our societal system (of color, white, young, old, etc.) affect us so that we can let go of the labels and move to living in the present. It is not to pretend or wish that our societal system does not label us; rather, it is to name and honor the labels that exist so that we can process how they have impacted us and, ultimately, move beyond them.

Benevolent Detachment: Because we live in a societal system that labels us many different ways (age, gender, sexual orientation, and so on), there are bound to be complexities, where one label intersects with another and thus leads to a different experience. Chapter 3 names ten major complexities, though certainly there are many more. Naming and understanding how these complexities impact us allows us to act out of benevolent detachment rather than reacting.

Practice: Chapter 4 gives us concrete tools to practice our awareness as individuals, within our organizations, and as a community. These tools invite us to see the diversity of experiences and opinions with our staff, in our families, and in the people we interact with as strengths to build upon.

CHAPTER 1

AWARENESS

BECOMING CONSCIOUS OF OUR EXPERIENCE AND PERSPECTIVE WITHIN THE SOCIETAL SYSTEM

Within our twenty-first century world of diverse experiences and opinions, there is a growing understanding that our personal experiences directly impact our perception of and interactions with others. An awareness of our individual perceptions is required for us to be effective in various spheres of our lives. For some of us, our jobs require this awareness. For others, the need for awareness is more personal as our families grow more diverse than ever before. For many, the value of this awareness is interwoven with beliefs relating to morals, religious faith, or the pursuit for social justice.

Whether in professional or personal circles, working with diversity (of age, gender, economic class, race, sexual orientation, and so on) can challenge us. We will be in situations where we observe others' behaviors, actions, or responses and ask ourselves, "Where are they coming from? Why would they do (or say) that?"

When we observe things that we do not understand from our experiences, we often do one of two things: judge what we are seeing or react to it. Both prevent us from being the most effective supervisor, first responder, educator, religious leader, volunteer, health care professional, judge, lawyer, business person, or family member possible.

> When working in the social services field, I witnessed variations on the following scenario repeatedly. A new employee conducted a home visit with a family living in generational poverty in a predominately poor neighborhood. The staffer returned to the office before the hour session should have been over voicing judgments about the family. "If they're living in poverty and need our services, how can they afford a big-screen TV? Why don't they use their money on something more important?" When I asked him why he had returned to the office so soon, he responded, "I didn't feel comfortable." To clarify, I asked if he had felt physically threatened. "No," he replied. "I just don't get the big-screen TV and stuff." The staffer saw something (the big-screen TV) that he did not understand, judged the family, and reacted by leaving early. The reaction and judgment resulted in the staffer not being as effective as possible in that home visit.

When we try to cover up the judgments we hold, it rarely works. Speaking and acting professionally doesn't necessarily mask our disapproval. Most people are aware when they are being judged and they immediately become defensive or disengaged. The interaction then becomes stunted and ineffective.

| Awareness of Our Experience | + | Openness to Another Experience | = | Opportunity to Be Heard |

In order to understand others, we must first analyze our own experiences and become aware of how they shape the manner in which we view, react, and behave in society. Obviously, every individual experiences life differently. For instance, ask a person who is right-hand dominant if tools, light switches, doors, sporting equipment, and everyday items work well for her. A person who is right-handed might answer a perplexed "yes," followed by asking, "Why wouldn't they work?" But ask a person who is left-hand dominate if those items work for him and the response will likely be a resounding, "No!"

Even siblings who grew up in the same household will recall family events in their own way. I guarantee that some of my family memories and my perception of how those events shaped my life are recalled differently by my siblings. Their memories are no more right or wrong than my recollection of events. Likewise, the experience of a person who is right-hand dominant is no more or less valid than the experience of a person who is left-hand dominant. People experience and perceive events differently.

Our own experiences are the lens through which we see the world. For example, if you were raised by an alcoholic parent, that experience shaped you. If you are now a health care provider in an emergency-room setting, your feelings connected with being raised by an alcoholic parent may shape your professional encounters with alcoholics and their children. Some health care providers who personally experienced an alcoholic parent may be more understanding and compassionate to an alcoholic patient. Other health care providers who personally experienced an alcoholic parent may find painful memories stirred up when treating those who struggle with addiction. Thus, those providers may spend less time treating alcoholic patients or have terser interactions.

Though both health care providers may have had similar experiences growing up, how they perceive those experiences and how their perceptions affect them might be very different. Acknowledging that our experiences and perceptions uniquely shape us helps us move away from a "right versus wrong" attitude. Judging others' perceptions almost always limits our effectiveness, communication, and, ultimately, our success.

Effective communication does not necessarily occur only when all parties agree with each other, but when all parties feel heard. Research bears this out in interactions, ranging from marriage to the marketplace. (Schwartz, 2014) The business world has discovered that when customers feel that their voices count, product and company loyalty increases. (RightNow Technologies, 2010)

This collective desire to be heard requires someone to listen. Effective listening begins with an awareness of our experiences and how those experiences might affect our perceptions. It means an openness to understanding how others may experience and perceive (even the same) situations differently. It's not always easy; being open to hearing others can be difficult and exhausting.

> *Near the end of my career in the social service field, I was challenged by this openness. I supervised a large staff that included a group of young adults who would be considered millennials. Watching them constantly using their phones and computers during meetings baffled me. I perceived these young people as acting disrespectfully. Not*

appreciating that they searched for information online rather than asking seasoned individuals sitting at the table with them, I caught myself acting out of my judgment, glaring at them as they reached for their phones. In order to effectively supervise these young adults, I realized I had better understand their experience of the world. No doubt it wasn't the same as mine.

I started by examining my experience and how it affects my perception. I realized that I am a digital immigrant. (Cunningham, 2007) I did not grow up with technology, but had to learn to incorporate it into my world. Technology is not innately the first manner in which I try to access information. Calling someone to ask a question or reading a book to gather information appeals to me; it has been my primary experience of how to properly gather data. But to my younger colleagues, digital natives who grew up using technology, my way appears slow and outdated. Realizing this and owning my technology experience allowed me to be more open to others' experiences. Instead of reacting with offense as the young adults looked at their phones during meetings, I made a conscious effort to realize that our experiences were different; they did not understand their actions as rude. Without judgment (as much as humanly possible), we talked together about how to operate a meeting in a way that was productive and respectful for all.

Being aware of my experience, open to the staff's experiences, and reengaging in a conversation where I listened (not reacted out of my own experience) allowed us to find a more effective approach to conducting meetings. Effective communication helped everyone feel their opinions and experiences had been heard. We moved toward a solution together.

Feeling that we have been listened to conveys a sense of being respected. When we feel respected, we often perform our job duties better and interact with each other more effectively.

DISCUSSION

- When have you experienced conflict or misunderstandings because your experience and understanding of a situation was different from a coworker's or family member's experience?
- Consider disciplinary actions, grievance reports, suspensions, and firings at work. What role do you think different perspectives of the same events play in these conflict situations?
- We obviously can't know everyone's experiences and perspectives, so how can we position ourselves to be open to hearing others' viewpoints?
- Name three experiences that you believe have most impacted your perceptions in life. Examples might include significant relationships, how you were raised, the morals instilled in you, what you observed around you as a child, and so on.
- Imagine a scenario where you feel a store clerk has treated you rudely, so you complain to management. How will your reaction differ if you feel the manager listened to your

concern, contrasted with a conversation in which you feel the manager did not hear your complaint?

- How do you respond when you feel a coworker or family member does not really hear and understand you? How do you respond when you feel listened to? Then reverse the roles. How do your family members and co-workers respond when they do not feel heard by you? Think of a situation when someone not feeling heard has escalated conflict. How could it have been handled differently?

How we interact with others is naturally impacted by our personal experiences and perceptions. The institutions we work in, the communities we live and work in, and the policies that govern those communities can also affect how we experience and perceive ourselves and others. In order to maximize our efforts to become more effective, we will want to think systemically about our societal system and our experience within it.

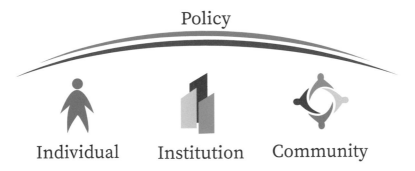

Societal System
Policy

Individual Institution Community

DEFINING THE SOCIETAL SYSTEM

The components of a society and the relationship between them form the societal system. Though there are many elements in a societal system, for simplification, we will focus on four major components of the societal system: individuals, organizations, communities, and policies.

You and I are individuals who live and interact within our societal system. We use or work or volunteer for organizations (such as businesses, police departments, churches, hospitals, schools, and big-box stores). We live in communities including local (neighborhood, town, or city), states or provinces, and nations. Policies and laws govern individual, organizational, and community components. Together, all four components and the interactions between them create our societal system.

Though we are affected by all parts of the societal system, we tend to see the world predominantly through the lens of one component, rather than systematically. For example, those whose jobs primarily involve individual interactions may tend to view the societal system primarily through the individual lens, inherently thinking about how the different components will impact the individual. Those among us who have made it to middle or executive management have likely picked up the organizational lens, furthering what is in the best interests of the organization as a whole. The folks working on community issues are often well aware of how a community's resources affect individuals and institutions, so they may migrate toward seeing the societal system through a community lens. Policies are created and altered by those imagining their ramifications through a policy lens.

INDIVIDUAL LENS

Naturally, an individual's primary lens (the lens a person tends to view the societal system with) can change over a lifetime, and even from situation to situation during the course of a day. Most of us are not even aware that we tend to look at the world through the lens of one component. Often, our personal experience impacts which component lens is primary in any given moment.

I started life viewing everything from the individual lens; it was my primary focus for years. It wasn't until I was well into my career and a manager that I began to understand things through an organizational lens. At one point, my decision to continue to live and survive in a high-poverty community helped me to see things through a community lens. And now as I near the end of my time, I often reflect how policies have impacted my life, both personally and professionally.

I'm a post-World War II baby. After my father developed tuberculosis, he was in and out of a tuberculosis sanatorium and was not able to be present for most of the first five years of my life. We first lived in a reservation town and then moved to Tucson, Arizona, which began our family's instability. My family's moves were never planned. They would simply happen—often without warning in the middle of the night.

I had attended eleven schools by the time I was in the ninth grade. My mother suffered from mental illness and my father was often not present on a daily basis. There was no significant parenting or direction that took place; we lived in survival mode. We were poor. Being poor, for me, meant living moment to moment. Chaos and drama were always present. We often couldn't pay the rent or our electricity would get turned off. I always felt that my people were living in a state of fear, waiting for the next crisis. That became my modus operandi.

I simply did not have any model other than the disorder and uncertainty of poverty. Following the pattern I knew, I acted out and became a delinquent. I lived a completely thoughtless and chaotic existence, in and out of juvenile centers and state psychiatric hospitals while taking every drug known to humankind.

At age 21, I found myself a single parent with two small children, holding an eviction notice with no clear options of what to do next. I had never done anything with a strategy. Planning wasn't a skill I had learned growing up in poverty. Without much physical or emotional stability, I simply reacted to what happened to and around me. The only way I knew to view or experience life was through the individual lens. It was all about me and those around me in the present. We did not think or act as if there was a tomorrow. Every decision was based on surviving in that moment.

To subsist at age 21 with two small children and no opportunities, I reluctantly applied for AFDC (Aid to Families with Dependent Children). Asking *for welfare humiliated me. I was assigned a team consisting of a social worker, a financial worker, and a job coach.*

The social worker came to my house and assessed my situation. Her expectations were that I finish high school and remain clean and sober. The financial worker helped me create a budget, something I had never known how to do. The job coach set up my schedule for school attendance and job preparation. I had never completed anything in my life, but it was made clear that I needed to participate in my own recovery. At that time, the system required real engagement between recipients and the organizational team.

I attended GED classes and graduated at the head of the class. This would not have been possible without the intense support of the social worker and the supervisor of the educational program. They were my first authentic teaching role models who motivated my life change.

Their expectations and demands were the first steps in my transformation from a person who merely reacted to what happened to a person who made choices based on future ramifications. Though I still viewed and experienced life through the individual lens, this skill set—the ability to imagine a different future and believe that I could shape it—helped me begin to see the world from an organizational lens.

ORGANIZATIONAL LENS

It took me eleven years to earn my GED and a bachelor's degree. Along the way, I worked in several organizations, slowly comprehending how to be effective at work. I recall that early in my work life, I thought I should be applauded for arriving at work on time four days in a row.

Though I was employed, I was still just trying to survive and was surrounded by people in similar conditions. When you are in survival mode, you can really only deal with that. Survival mode invites chaos; you can't afford maintenance on your car, so it's always breaking down. You can't afford regular daycare, so you have undependable sitters who cause you to miss work when they don't show up.

At first, I did not understand why my supervisor was upset that I was regularly late or that I asked for a few days off each month. A few excellent managers did not react to me and my lateness; rather, they listened. Then they explained the expectations of the work world and respectfully demanded that I meet them. Once I comprehended their focus through the organizational lens, I was able to advance in my career.

As years went by, I kept getting promoted. I began to truly understand the nature of organizational influence. Working my way up in a large social service agency, I became privy to the inside workings of services designed to meet the needs of people in deep poverty. Not only did I work for the organization that once assisted me, but I eventually oversaw their operations.

As a representative of the management team, I was expected to do what was best for the organization. I had to support decisions not always ideal for individuals that I knew would bring in revenue the organization needed to continue helping people. As I read the new stats and trends, I would consider how they would affect us as an organization. Though I tried to balance the individual and organizational needs, my job responsibilities mandated that my primary emphasis be the organization.

Viewing situations from the organizational lens allowed me to see the bigger picture rather than just individual behavior directly in front of me. For example, my duties on the lead management team meant I worked with high-ranking police representatives. I heard the demands their department was under to demonstrate they were actively policing and fighting crime. When I saw individuals in the neighborhood getting ticketed by police, I realized that officer was demonstrating to the department (organization) that the neighborhood was being actively policed. My lens had changed; previously, I would have seen this situation from the individual lens—as yet another person from our neighborhood being targeted by police. Now I could see both the organization demands and the individual components, as well as how they interacted.

The more I learned and the more influence I was given, the more I realized that the services the organization provided were often there to meet the needs of the organization, not the individual. We set up new programs without evidence of their effectiveness, but we knew they would generate the revenue needed for the organization, so we proceeded.

COMMUNITY LENS

For 25 years, I have lived in one of the poorest neighborhoods in my city. While the faces have changed, the issues of this fractured neighborhood remain. What has kept me here, well after I could afford to move out, was the effort of neighboring homeowners. They understood that in order for us to survive the chaos of poverty, we needed to make a long-term investment in community, even if it was only our little block. Thus, all of us have remained and view ourselves as true neighbors. We throw block parties four times a year and call across the fence to each other. We created community where there once was none. It is through this experience that I began to understand how important community is. It became my primary focus, though sometimes that has been challenging.

The agency where I was upper management received funding to put a "drop-in center" (a place where people who are unemployed or homeless can come to receive a meal and other services) in the community where I lived. For many who did not live in my community, this sounded like a wonderful idea—providing assets to both individuals and the neighborhoods. But for those of us living there, our perspective was different. Our little community wanted to bring in grocery stores, libraries, and other agencies that would help sustain us and increase our community capital. (Leyden, 2003) We did not welcome yet another program that would manage chaos and, as unintentional as it might be, decrease our community capital. Here, my organizational lens and community lens were at odds. I knew from an agency perspective that a drop-in center was an important resource. But through my community lens, it did not feel like something that would better us. When I brought my concerns to a management meeting, I was surprised by how many fellow managers never considered the issue from the perspective of the people actually living in the neighborhood. It was shocking how many managers could not acknowledge that those of us within the community held different perspectives on the proposed development.

POLICY LENS

The experience of having created community in order to survive allowed me to view the world through the community lens. My quest for understanding created many questions. Why do our communities look so different? How do we as a community get more resources? The answers to these questions helped me see the world through a policy lens.

I recall going to visit friends at their new house in a new upper-middle-class development. As I drove through the community, I quickly noticed the many walking paths, well-kept parks, open green spaces, large lots, and nicely paved streets, as well as an absence of billboards. All the housing was in one area and all the stores in another area; the distance between the areas was drivable but not walkable. I thought of how different the zoning laws, planning permits, and housing regulations (all policies) in this neighborhood must be compared to my neighborhood. I couldn't help but think that policies influence how we develop areas and how the businesses we allow to be present within those areas affect the residents' sense of community.

The GI Bill of 1944, a policy by way of federal legislation, gave World War II veterans unprecedented access to college, trade schools, and guaranteed home loans.[1] However, most people of color who served in WWII did not receive the GI Bill benefits. (Katznelson, 2005) For many urban communities, this meant white male vets were able to move out of the city into the first-ring suburbs, purchasing houses with larger lots in neighborhoods with newer schools, more parks, and better infrastructure.[2] Left behind were families of color who often did not make the same wage as their white counterparts. (Turner & Bound, 2003) Urban communities' resources were often depleted during this time as the tax base dropped. My realization as to why my community looked and operated the way it did was understood more clearly through the wide view of a historical policy lens.

As I reflect on my life, I also can see the effect that policies have had on me as an individual, the organizations I have worked for, and the community in which I live. For instance, as a beneficiary of President Lyndon Johnson's War on Poverty policies, I was able to attend the University of Minnesota.[3] While I worked and attended class, my children received excellent daycare. When I worked for a social service agency implementing programs, the organization was influenced by the policies the state and federal government mandated to us. Likewise, my community was subject to local, state, and federal policies that impacted how the neighborhood looked and functioned.

As stated previously, I have used the four different lenses (individual, organizational, community, and policy) to view the world around me. One is not better than the other and none were necessarily intentional. In my experience, being able to view a situation through all four lenses is a valuable tool. When issues arise, this approach tends to address the entire problem, not just one part of it.

Acknowledging Our Primary Component within the Societal System	+	Intentionally Viewing the Societal System as a Whole	=	More Comprehensive Awareness

DISCUSSION

- Through which of the four lenses are you most likely to view the world?
- Compare your lens now to another time in your life when your lens was different. What factors do you think caused your primary lens to change?
- How do you think your current primary lens affects how you view situations at work, in the news, and within your personal relationships?
- A difference in perception can invariably trigger conflict. How do you listen to others when you must collaborate with someone who sees things through a different lens? For example, when a front-line employee sees a situation from an individual lens, but the manager's perspective is clearly influenced from an organizational lens, how do you reconcile those to work toward a common goal?
- How might naming the lenses through which you typically see the world change your interactions? What surprises you about labeling how you predominantly see the world?
- The adage about working hard to get ahead in life focuses on the individual. Of course, some people work very hard and still don't get ahead. How can that adage be reframed for an organization, community, or policy? For instance, minimum-wage policies can affect the outcome of someone's hard work, the availability of banks and quality medical care impacts a hard-working person, and so on. Change the individually focused "works hard" element in the sentence to reflect different lenses: "A person who _____ can get ahead." (Examples include "has medical

insurance," "has subsidized child care," "has reliable transportation," and so on.) Identify which lens (individual, community, organizational, policy) each fits in.

THINKING SYSTEMICALLY

Understanding our perspective and being aware of the perspectives of others will require that we think systemically. This means we look at how the societal system operates, not just as components (individual, organization, community, and policy), but as a whole. It means we understand that one part affects all the parts in the system. We are stepping out of our experiences at work, at home, and in community to examine the system in its entirety.

We are, so to speak, looking at the entire forest instead of an individual tree. Thinking systemically does not mean we ignore the individual components, but that we observe how they interact and react to each other and how that affects the system as a whole.

"If we want to solve problems effectively . . . we must keep in mind not only many features but also the influences among them." — *Deitrich Dörner. (Dörner, 1997)*

Thinking systemically is realizing that every individual, organization, community, and policy happens within a system. The system affects the parts and the parts affect each other as well as the system as a whole.

For example, in the systemic diagram, the dot in the individual circle represents a person with diabetes. Some individuals make unhealthy choices that increase their diabetic risk. Other individuals make healthy choices to lower their risk, but due to circumstances out of their control, they are diabetic. Many countries have seen an explosion in the number of diabetes diagnoses. In response, organizations have created more diabetes programs. Social service agencies and health clinics have set up classes on managing diabetes. The individual diabetic affects the organization and community. In return, the organization and community affect the individual.

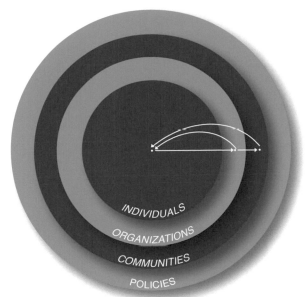

INDIVIDUALS

ORGANIZATIONS

COMMUNITIES

POLICIES

As we view diabetes systemically, we must also look at how policies impact its prevalence. For instance, community economic and zoning policies influence retail development including the number and type of food sources present. Public transit availability affects access to reasonably priced fresh food. (Mead, 2008) When healthy, affordable groceries are difficult to obtain and there is a lower ratio of parks and recreation opportunities for residents in urban neighborhoods, the scenario for a significant public health predicament has been created.

On the organizational level, some government policies have encouraged the rise of processed foods. Subsidized commodities such as corn syrup have contributed to the epidemic of obesity and diabetes. (Fields, 2004) At the same time, the system has experienced a larger demand for food as human population increases. ("Population Clock." n.d.) Thus, different farming entities emerge; communities change as small farms disappear and large, corporate farms, which tend to be more dependent on chemicals and genetically altered produce and animals, flourish. (Dimitri, Effland, & Conklin, 2005)

These policy changes ultimately impact many individuals' food options, the overall economies of communities, the environment of our planet, and individuals' life expectancy.

THE SYSTEMIC WEB

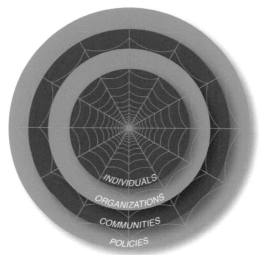

Thinking systemically becomes like inspecting a spider web. Pulling one thread of the web affects the other threads and anchors, which then affect the interconnected web as a whole.

It is often our human inclination to view situations and information through one of the components (individual, organization, community, or policy) within the societal system, rather than viewing it systemically. As we work toward unlocking our full personal and professional potential, we will begin to understand the societal system as a whole.

GROUP WORK: OPTION 1

View the documentary series *Unnatural Causes…Is Inequality Making Us Sick?* (https://unnaturalcauses.org/)
If time is limited, prioritize watching Season 1, Episode 5: "Place Matters."

DISCUSSION

- How do health-related problems impact individuals, organizations, communities, and policies?
- Regarding health issues, what, if anything, is the responsibility of the individual, the organization, the community, and policy?
- How are health issues in the profiled communities a systemic problem? In other words, how does each of the four components of the system (individual, organization, community, and policy) impact health issues there?
- Do you recognize any parallels in your community?

GROUP WORK: OPTION 2

View the Independent Lens documentary *The House I Live In* (2013), directed by Eugene Jarecki.

DISCUSSION

- How do illegal drug problems impact individuals, organizations, communities, and policies?
- Regarding illegal drugs, what, if anything, is the responsibility of the individual, the organization, the community, and policy?

- How are illegal drugs and the war on them a systemic problem?
- Do you recognize any parallels to the video in your community?

HOMEWORK

- Take a recent article from a newspaper in your area or listen to a specific news story. From which lens (individual, organization, community, or policy) was the news story reported? Why do you think that is?
- All four components (individual, organization, community, and policy) are part of every story. How could you rewrite or report on the news story from above to intentionally demonstrate how all four components played a role?
- Challenge yourself to reflect systemically on a situation at work or in the world. View it from all four lenses. How do your feelings or reactions about the situation change from each viewpoint? Which is most helpful to the situation?

CHAPTER 2

INFLUENCE

ANALYZING HOW NORMALIZATION AFFECTS OUR
EXPERIENCES, PERSPECTIVES, AND EFFECTIVENESS

Our societal system regularly normalizes one particular thing or group over another. When something becomes normalized, the societal system (individuals, organizations, communities, and policies) creates supports for that which has become normalized. When one group has all four components geared toward it, that group will receive inherent benefits. To illustrate normalization and the benefits that one receives as part of the normalized group, let's revisit the right-hand dominant/left-hand dominant discussion. Has your country normalized being right-handed or left-handed?

In most countries, including the United States, being right-handed is normalized. (Eveleth, 2013) The societal system is geared toward right-handers. This is reflected even in communication. Most languages in the world associate the word "left" with a negative bias; root word associations include meanings such as broken, untrustworthy, awkward, and wrong. (Kushner, 2013) The Oxford Dictionary's online definition of "left-handed" includes the meaning "perverse." ("Definition of Left-Handed by Lexico," n.d.) Though it's difficult to know the exact source of this bias against lefties, many speculate that it's related to the left hand being the "unclean" hand in many cultures. Because hand-washing isn't always readily available, after toileting, the left hand is used for cleaning oneself. That leaves the right hand for other activities, including eating. In a culture still following this practice (of which there are many), extending the left hand in greeting sends a rather clear message. Whatever the reason, bias against the left hand and its dominant users goes back at least a couple of thousand years. (Kushner, 2013)

Our societal system is geared toward being right-handed. Consider what benefits people who are right-handed receive. If you are right-handed, it may be difficult for you to list these benefits. Many things are geared toward you, so you probably haven't had to be aware that left-handers have not had the same experience. This is the rule of normalization: if you are part of a group that has been normalized, it is naturally more difficult to realize the benefits you have. You haven't had to think about it. Your experience is that things just worked and your perception is likely that the same is probably true for all people. However, a person who is left-hand dominant can often list several benefits that people who are right-hand dominant receive because people who are left-handed have had to experience a societal system that has not been geared for them. When a societal system is not geared toward you, you are aware that some things just do not work; you must adapt as you attempt to live successfully within the system because the system is not adapted to you.

Besides scissors, school desks, sporting equipment, and guitars geared toward right-handers, people who are left-handed usually can list benefits of other items that many right-handed people aren't aware of: can openers, slot machines, levers on reclining chairs, door handle and light switch locations, cooking equipment, ironing boards and irons, bowling balls, the computer mouse and keyboard, phones, and cameras. Left-handers know that instructions, such as how to crochet and how to tie shoelaces, are usually geared for right-handers. Manufacturers typically design equipment for a right-handed person including power tools such as chainsaws and the safety on firearms. Store credit-card readers often have a slide slot on the right side so it is easier to use if you are right-handed. Men's single-pocket business shirts often place the pocket on the left side so it is easily accessible for a right-handed person. American Sign Language is right-hand dominant. The list goes on and on.

Right-handed people might be blissfully unaware of some of the examples above. This is not to say that right-handers are to blame for the benefits they receive being part of the normalized group or for left-handers' experiences. The benefits are intrinsically woven into a right-handed person's existence. However, if one is part of the group that is not normalized (as a left-hander experiences), awareness of the benefits one has not received are easier to recognize out of necessity because the left-hander has been forced to adjust.

In order to be the most effective people in both the personal and professional realms, we must become aware of our individual experience within the societal system and examine how it may affect our perception. Being aware means that we acknowledge when we have been part of the normalized group and when we have not. Once we are more aware of our experience, we can begin to process how our experience within the societal system affects us and be open to hearing how it may affect others.

The culmination of this understanding is to inherently recognize that normalization in societal systems exists, that we each are a part of it, and that it impacts us and our organizations. Our personal awareness of living in a societal system in which normalization exists allows us to be open to understanding others' experiences and to realize they are not the same as our own. Because many of our jobs require that we teach, supervise, work with, case manage, or police people who have experienced the societal system differently than we have, this understanding can greatly increase our efficacy so that we don't find ourselves reacting to the very people with whom we want to work for. We will be able to better recognize when we are acting out of our experience and reacting to other's actions simply due to people experiencing a societal system differently. For instance, recall Allison's illustration of working with the millennial staff and how she reacted to their constant use of phones during a meeting. When she became aware of her experience in the societal system and was open to their experiences, she was able to work more effectively with them.

Where do we start? We begin the process by becoming aware of what is normalized in our societal system. Remember, normalization means that all four components (individuals, organizations, communities, and policies), at one time or another, were geared toward a specific group.

Normalization is not necessarily the same as being part of the majority. Obviously, being part of the majority means that you are part of a group that is more numerous than other groups. But sometimes the minority is normalized, having all four components geared toward it and benefitting from it.

For example, during the apartheid years in South Africa, the minority white population was normalized, despite being about a fifth of the total population. Because preferential treatment was given to whites in policy and practice, the majority population was not the normalized group.

As you consider what it means to be part of the normalized group, remember that policies do not necessarily have to be currently geared toward the normalized. Rather, the four components (individuals, organizations, communities, and policies) had to, at one time, have been geared toward one specific group. Over time, policies are often changed to move toward equality. But even when policies change and are geared toward equalization, the effects of the past normalization endure.

The people of South Africa overthrew apartheid in 1993 and as a result, the country's policies have changed dramatically. Yet even with policy changes and people of color continuing to be the majority population (as well as holding the presidency), whites still earn higher wages, own more land, have a higher standard of living, and outlive their black counterparts. (Leibbrandt, Levinsohn, and McCrary, 2005) Changes in normalization can be very slow, even taking hundreds of years. Even dramatic shifts in policy change do not automatically change the status quo of what is societally normalized. People who have had the benefits of being part of the normalized group will often continue to do so, long after policies have equalized.

The Triangle Chart

Each triangle represents a group. A triangle on its base pointing upward represents a normalized group. A triangle pointing downward represents a group that is not normalized. For example, one triangle pointing up is labeled "right-handed," a group that is normalized. The triangle pointing down adjacent to it is labeled "left-handed," a group that is not normalized.

On the following pages, you will see a chart with eighteen normalized groups (triangle pointing up) and eighteen groups that are not normalized (triangle pointing down). Following the Triangle Chart, you will see a table where the full names of each group are listed and a brief definition of the identities given. A similar table can be found in the index. Also included are citations and examples of how the normalized group still receives benefits, validating that it is a normalized group. Remember: individuals, organizations, communities, or policies once were (or currently are) geared toward a specific group in order for it to qualify as being a normalized group.

Some of the names used to identify groups may be unfamiliar to you, especially in the non-normalized categories. Names are important! They are a means by which we acknowledge each other; without having a name that reflects a group you belong to, you may feel invisible or discounted. Excluding a group or using derogatory or inaccurate names thwarts our effectiveness immediately. In forming this book, Allison and I have worked very hard to avoid that mistake.

After gathering feedback from several groups and listening to many viewpoints, we very intentionally tried to use names that accurately identify people in both normalized and non-normalized groups. Nonetheless, when tackling complex categories and having to pick a single name to identify an entire group, it was sometimes difficult to do justice to our intentions. With this admission, we ask that you use the names given in your discussion group and as you complete the activities.

I understand that it is impossible to list all groups. For example, there are more than six thousand spoken languages in the world. Due to the simplification of the triangle chart, it would be unfeasible to list all languages. Because of the context in which this book is presented, the non-normalized triangle was labeled as "C, S, H, A," which on the following page you see stands for Chinese, Spanish, Hindi, and Arabic. There is an intentional use of some of the most broadly used languages in the world to represent many when they could not all be named. We apologize for our limitations.

As you review the triangle chart, the listing of the names of other groups may seem tedious, politically correct, foreign, or frustrating. I have lived a long enough life that I have seen some of the names change, new ones added, and people asking to be identified by different designations. Trying to keep up with the terms by which every group identifies can feel exhausting or overly sensitive. But one thing I have learned is that we cannot be successful in our work if we do not acknowledge one another. The fact that I have the benefit of belonging to groups whose names were already known motivates me to learn the names of groups that frequently go unnamed. Remember that everyone in our communities, in our professional world, and in our personal world wants to be heard.

As you read the names, please note there is a difference between a name being inaccurate and feeling uncomfortable with a name. For example, when Allison was diagnosed with terminal pancreatic cancer, her health declined. She became part of the upside-down triangle that refers to a person with a disability. She hated admitting that she was part of that group; it infuriated her! It wasn't that the name was inaccurate—her body matched the definition. But she grieved losing the benefits that accompany being a person without disability. She had to process experiencing the societal system in a new way, a way that made her uncomfortable. But she acknowledged that it didn't change the fact that a non-normalized group exists for people with disabilities. And though she struggled to accept being part of a group she didn't want to be in, she knew that placing herself in that group was accurate. Check your discomfort level as you work through the triangles and consider what might be triggering it.

TRIANGLE CHART
My Experience with the Societal System

IDENTITY	DEFINITION
Right-Handed	**Right-Handed**: A person who primarily uses his or her right hand to complete tasks.
Left-Handed	**Left-Handed**: A person who primarily uses his or her left hand to complete tasks.
Middle Class Upper-Middle Upper Class	**Middle Class, Upper-Middle, Upper Class**: Earning the median income or above in your country.
Underclass	**Underclass**: Working full-time or more and earning an income below the median income in your country.
Working Poor	**Working Poor**: Working for an income that is below the median income in your country.
Impoverished	**Impoverished**: Earning an income in lowest quarter of your country's income.
Male	**Male**: A person who has one or more of the following: internal and/or external organs that are intended to produce sperm, one Y chromosome, testosterone (sex hormone) at levels appropriate for age.
Female	**Female**: A person who has one or more of the following: internal organs that are intended to produce ovum, two X chromosomes, estrogen and progesterone (sex hormones) levels appropriate for age.
Intersex	**Intersex**: A person who has a variation in sex characteristics, including chromosomes, gonads, or genitals that do not allow the individual to be distinctly identified as male or female. Such variation may involve genital ambiguity or a combination of chromosomal genotype and sexual phenotype other than XY male and XX female.
Able-Body	**Able-Body**: A body that is able to move and be fully functional with few to no limitations and with little to no assistance.
Person with Physical Disability	**Person with Physical Disability**: A body that may be limited in movement and function and/or requires assistance to increase functionality.
Able-Minded	**Able-Minded**: A human mind that is able to receive, compute, and process information and/or feelings.
Person with Disability	**Person with Disability**: A human mind that is compromised in its ability to receive, compute, and process information and/or feelings.
White	**White**: Race is a social construct without biological meaning. It has been used to separate human beings based on the "color" or amount of pigment in their skin. A person who appears White will have a lesser level of melanocyte cellular activity. And have external physical characteristics that reflect a dominant European ancestry.
Of Color	**Of Color**: Race is a social construct without biological meaning. It has been used to separate human beings based on the "color" or amount of pigment in their skin. A person Of Color will have a higher level of melanocyte cellular activity. They will be a person whose external physical characteristics reflect Indigenous or Aboriginal ancestry from the Americas, aboriginal, African, Asian, Pacific Islands, and/or Middle Eastern.

IDENTITY   DEFINITION

Heterosexual

Heterosexual: A male sexually oriented to a female, or a female sexually oriented to a male.

Lesbian

Lesbian: A female sexually oriented to a female.

Gay

Gay: An individual sexually oriented to the same sex.

Bi-Sexual

Bi-Sexual: An individual sexually oriented to both males and females.

Pansexual

Pansexual: An individual sexually oriented to a person regardless of sex or gender identity.

Questioning

Questioning: An individual currently in the process of determining what his or her sexual orientation is.

Asexual

Asexual: An individual who has no sexual desire or activity.

Christianity

Christianity: Monotheistic faith that emerged from Judaism based on the teachings of Jesus as the son of God and Messiah.

Islam

Islam: The monotheistic faith of Muslims based on the teachings of the prophet Muhammad to surrender to the will of Allah.

Hinduism

Hinduism: A faith in a supreme God with many deities with a system of values known as dharma with an emphasis on reincarnation of the soul.

Agnosticism

Agnosticism: Belief that human reason is incapable of providing sufficient proof to determine if God does or does not exist.

Buddhism

Buddhism: Based upon the teachings of Siddhartha Gautama with varying rituals, customs, and beliefs. All centering on seeking enlightenment and ending suffering.

Atheism

Atheism: Belief that there is no god or gods.

Sikhism

Sikhism: Monotheistic religion that seeks daily devotion and remembrance of God at all times through acts of service and charity that earn the believer a place with God.

Judaism

Judaism: monotheistic religion based on the teachings of the Torah with an emphasis of showing devotion to God by following God's laws in all aspects of life.

English-Formal Register

English-Formal Register: Grammatically correct, proper English, used in professional and formal settings.

Chinese

Chinese: A group of languages used in China and surrounding area the most popular dialect being Mandarin.

Spanish

Spanish: The language of Spain, Mexico and many Latin American countries

Hindi

Hindi: An Indic Language of northern India, derived from Sanskirt and written in the Devanagari script.

IDENTITY   DEFINITION

Arabic

Arabic: Southern-Central Semitic language spoken in parts of the Middle East, North Africa and most of the Arabian Peninsula.

Portuguese

Portuguese:Romance language that is spoken in Portugal, Brazil and other Portuguese colonial and formerly colonial territories.

Informal English

Informal English: asual English language used typically among friends and in informal settings or communications; may utilize grammatically incorrect phrases or slang. Has grammatically incorrect sentence structure and typically uses less vocabulary than formal English. (Note: accents do not determine if one is using formal or informal English.)

Formally Educated

Formally Educated: A person who has completed the requirements to obtain a certification or degree from an accredited learning or higher-education institution.

Informally Educated

Informally Educated: A person whose knowledge is acquired through life experiences and/or previous employment.
reflect a dominant European heritage.

Employed

Employed: An individual who is working or has a role that allows that person to meet his or her basic needs (food, housing, transportation).

Unemployed

Unemployed: A person who is not working.

Underemployed

Underemployed: A person who is working but unable to meet his or her basic needs.

Married

Married: A person who is in a legally binding relationship, recognized by the government.

Single

Single: A person who is not in a union with another person.

Partnered but Unmaried

Partnered but Unmarried: A person who is in a union that is not legally recognized.

Divorced

Divorced: A person who once was married whose legal union is now dissolved.

Widowed

Widowed: A person whose legally married spouse has passed away.

Age 18-65

Age 18-65: A person who has lived more than 18 years and less than 65 years. The age of 65 is a fluid number. As one ages they start to become invisible and as sources state discriminated against. Of course this may start when one is 64 or not until 70 years of age. Thus, 65 years of age is not an absolute.

Under Age 18

Under Age 18: a person who has lived less than 18 years. 18 years of age is an absolute. Rarely does the societal system allow for those under 18 years of age to have their voices heard or given power within institutions, communities and at a policy level. In the United States of America upon turning 18 you have the right to vote, you begin to have more opportunities for you voice to be heard within the societal system.

Over Age 65

Over Age 65: A person who has lived more than 65 years.

IDENTITY   DEFINITION

Have Children

Have Children: Have experienced legal responsibility for parenting a child under the age of eighteen.

Have No Children

Having No Children: No experience with legal responsibility for parenting a child under the age of eighteen.

Cisgender

Cisgender: A person's biological gender matches the gender identity and expression associated with that gender.

Transgender

Transgender: A person feels that his or her biological gender does not match the gender identity and expression associated with that gender but identifies or expresses himself or herself from the gender opposite his or her biological gender.

Gender Neutral

Gender Neutral: Not identifying with or expressing oneself from either gender.

Gender Fluid

Gender Fluid: Expressing oneself or identifying with either gender or with no specific gender or with a combination of identities.

Gender Diverse

Gender Diverse: Not conforming to traditional gender roles.

Non Binary Gender

Non Binary Gender: Is a spectrum of gender identities that are not exclusively masculine or exclusively feminine-identities that are outside gender binary.

Documented

Documented: A person possessing papers recognizing legal resident status of the country he or she resides in.

Undocumented

Undocumented: A person lacking legal papers legitimizing residential status of the country he or she resides in.

Underdocumented

Underdocumented. A a person possessing papers recognizing legal resident status of the country he or she resides in. But not having enough paper work to receive all benefits of full citizenship. For example, one may have a work visa which allows them to legally live and work in that country but does not allow them to collect aide such as social security.

European Ethnicity

European Ethnicity: Having or identifying with a majority of language, customs, religion, and/or physical characteristics related to heritage from European countries.

NA, A, A, H, A, PI, ME Ethnicity

NA, A, A, H, A, PI, ME Ethnicity: having or identifying with a majority of language, customs, religion, and/or physical characteristics related to heritage from one or more of the following areas: Native or tribal North American, Aboriginal, African, Hispanic, Asian, Pacific Islander, and Middle Eastern.

No or Minimal Criminal Record

No or Minimal Criminal Record: Having little or no significant record of civil or criminal breach of law. Previous infractions do not limit access to such things as voting, housing, food, and/or employment. Examples may include speeding tickets and underage drinking.

Criminal Background

Criminal Background: Having a legal record of significant civil or criminal breach of law. Previous crimes limit your access to such things as voting, housing, food, and/or employment.

Gender diverse ← any one gender but do things more low men to other. Tom-Boy

39

GROUP WORK

The previous pages will be your reference for discussion. The triangle chart contains eighteen sets of triangles. The following charts name each identity found in the triangles and give a brief definition. Sources and citations that demonstrate the benefits for the normalized group can be found in a chart in the index.

DISCUSSION

- What identities within the triangle chart are new to you? What identities are most familiar? What reactions (if any) do you have to those that are unfamiliar?

- How does identifying the groups assist in your work or your personal life? For example, in your profession, are you statistically likely to interact with people who represent every group? How does knowing about the groups and having had time to process thoughts and feeling increase effectiveness at work? How does your awareness diminish the burden of someone needing to educate you on his/her identity?

- We live in a societal system where these identities and normalization of other identities exist. Ultimately, we do not want to perpetuate normalization. Still, we cannot move beyond it until we acknowledge what exists. Our awareness begins with naming what exists so we can consciously process how it impacts us, our loved ones, and co-workers. Have you ever heard someone say, "I don't see color," or another identity? How might this statement feel for people who have experienced something different? How is naming what exists so we can come together to collectively talk about how to move beyond a more effective action?

Acknowledging the Identities We Hold	+	Processing How Those Identities Impact Our Future	=	A New Understanding of Our Perception

ACTIVITY

Look at the eighteen sets of triangles on the following chart. Thinking only of who you are today, circle the triangle that best describes you. Don't consider who you were yesterday, or when you were growing up, or even who you want to be in a month, a year, or five years from now. Think only of who you are at this moment. For example, the first triangle set is a choice of either right-handed or left-handed. Circle the triangle that best represents who you are today: right- or left-handed. The next triangle set is a choice of middle, upper middle, and upper class or underclass, working poor, and impoverished. For instance, if you grew up in poverty but at this moment would most accurately describe yourself as middle class, circle that triangle.

When you complete this activity, you should have eighteen circles. Absolutely there are ambiguous identities we hold. People's lives are complicated and the triangle exercise will reflect that. But we challenge you to ensure you circle all or some of the normalized triangle identities if you receive the benefits from that group's identity. If you currently hold an identity found in the inverted triangle but prefer a different or more specific description, please add it. For example, we use "of color" to include all people who are not white, but if you prefer BI-POC (black, indigenous- people of color) please add it. If you do not currently hold an identity found in the inverted triangle, we ask that you use the identity as it is written.

A participant once completing this activity spoke to us and it was obvious she had full command of formal English to express herself.

Still, she had what many Americans would consider a slight accent. She stated her first language was Hindi, but she had learned formal English at a young age at her private school. She knew she had all the benefits of speaking English fluently, but due to her accent, she was sometimes perceived as being part of the group not normalized and treated as such. She circled the entire normalized triangle with the English Formal identity but also circled a corner of the triangle with C, S, H, A, P, as her experience was partially aligned with that group. She felt that honored that she had most of the benefits of normalization while also acknowledging she occasionally did not.

Whether you are reading this as an individual or within a group, you will want to remind yourself that what one person circles is not better or worse than what another circles. We must be willing to step back from judgments such as right or wrong, positive or negative. All people have experienced events that have negatively impacted them, just as all humans have experienced events that have positively impacted them. The triangles you circle do not indicate if you had positive or negative experiences; they acknowledge that your individual experiences will be different from others' experiences.

For example, you might circle "right-handed," "middle class," and "female." If someone you work with circles "left-handed," "poverty," and "male," there certainly may be times when you will view the same situation differently. The point is to acknowledge that our individual experiences of the societal system differ. The way we experience the societal system often impacts how we are viewed, reacted to, and treated and also how we view, react to, and treat others. Understanding this will increase our effectiveness when dealing with individuals and groups whose experiences are different than ours.

Becoming aware of our experience within the societal system—regardless of which triangle we identify with—can evoke strong reactions. When working with groups, I have found that it can be difficult for some to realize that they have received societal benefits for no other reason than that they are part of a normalized group. A few may refuse to believe this; some who have experienced a lot of normalized triangles may feel guilty, frustrated, or even angry.

Be cognizant of the reaction, thoughts, or feelings this activity provokes. For example, I have occasionally observed that participants who have circled many normalized triangles start to feel guilty. Rather than acknowledging that feeling, processing it, and engaging in a conversation with people who have had other experiences, they often want to act out of the feeling of guilt and "fix" the benefit that is geared toward the normalized group. They react to left-handed people and other groups that represent the downward-pointing triangles with the equivalent of, "Oh, I didn't know that the credit card scanner at the checkout was geared for me and difficult for you. We will get that fixed immediately. Don't you worry; I'll call someone and make it fair." Moving to action can sometimes unintentionally steal the voice of the very group whose experience we are trying to understand. For left-handers, for instance, this may feel insulting, intrusive, or disrespectful.

On the other hand, people who have circled a lot of triangles representing a group that is not normalized may have feelings of frustration, denial, and even anger. "Sometimes it is so frustrating that I always have to adjust to the system! The system is never geared toward me. I try so hard to stay polite, but sometimes it is exhausting," said a left-handed person in my audience. Other left-handed people may have tried to adapt and assimilate for so long that they now feel uncomfortable talking about the difference.

There will be a broad range of experiences, thoughts, and feelings about any given triangle.

Feelings are part of the human condition. This work can certainly trigger some emotional reactions for you and others in your group, including an anxiety at acknowledging differences. Create a space where people can feel safe to express their feelings and where differences of experience and viewpoints are treated with respect. When talking, always assume someone in your group identifies with the triangle that you are talking about.

DISCUSSION

- Looking at what you circled on your triangle chart, what are your first impressions? What thoughts, emotions, or reactions did you experience in this process that you can identify?
- When was it difficult to decide which triangle to circle? When did you find yourself wishing you could circle the other triangle? Why?
- Did you have a sense of one triangle being "right" and the other being "wrong?" How could this affect your ability to relate to others in the workplace and in relationships?
- How can incorporating knowledge and mindfulness of what is normalized and what is not normalized improve our interpersonal and professional interactions?
- Choose five triangles that you did not circle. For example, if you are a female, heterosexual, middle class, informally educated, and Christian, you could think of a male, wealthy, gay, educated, Buddhist. How might his experiences differ from yours at work, in hailing a cab, picking a preschool for a child, finding a spiritual leader, and so on?
- As individuals, we don't necessarily automatically consider the experience of others in life. How might thinking through

the societal experiences of others make us more effective in our professional roles, in our personal lives? How is it for you to talk about your experience to others?

- If you have less than three non-normalized groups circled, how might this impact how you effectively supervise or relate to people who would circle more than three non-normalized triangles? If you have more than three non-normalized triangles circled, how might this impact how you effectively supervise or relate to people who would circle less than three non-normalized triangles? What do you have to be aware of, if anything? How do you adjust, if at all?

- How easy or difficult would you guess it is for someone to explain his or her non-normalized experience to someone whose experience is normalized? Which triangle categories would be especially difficult?

- Some participants might complete this exercise not wanting to acknowledge that differences exist. How can denial of different experiences within the societal system inhibit our personal and professional effectiveness and successes?

- Consider a time in your life when you connected with someone who experienced the world in a very different manner from you. How did that experience change you? How does having a loved one in a non-normalized group affect your understanding when you are part of the normalized group?

HOMEWORK

Choose a conversation or an action made this week at work, at home, or in an outside setting. It could be a conversation or decision made from a meeting with clients, talking with co-workers, an exchange at a local store with an employee, or a conversation with a family member. Replay the conversation, but flip some of their triangles (as you perceive them) and overlay different identities on the other person. How could flipping several triangles change the interaction or outcome of decisions made?

For example, a police department acknowledged that officers working at a large event outside in high temperatures all day were at risk of overheating. The administration wanted their officers to be as comfortable as possible, yet still adhere to the proper dress code. They got approval for and purchased short-sleeved male polo shirts for all the officers working this event. When the department distributed the shirts, many female officers did not have the excitement their male co-workers had with the shirts they were given. Why?

The administration was absolutely trying to be helpful and thought they were supporting their officers. However, the perception that polo shirts would be more comfortable was made by male police officers. They had not taken into consideration that bullet proof vests fit a woman's body differently, increasing the circumference of the chest. Male polo shirts are designed for flat chests, so female officers were left to decide whether to wear constrictive shirts that would ride up at the waist or shirts that were oversized and not in line with dress code regulations.

When processing your own example, try not to get into a conversation about right versus wrong or debate the details. Rather, discuss that because we all act out of the experiences we have had, more experiences at the table can create more effective actions.

This homework exercise should help us be more aware of our personal experiences in the societal system and more conscious of how experiences may differ for others.

CHAPTER 3

IMPACT

UNDERSTANDING THE COMPLEXITIES FOUND WITHIN A
SOCIETAL SYSTEM AND THE POWER OF NORMALIZATION

Once a group within the societal system becomes normalized, complexities arise. Complexities are the intricate ways elements within the societal system change because of the normalization that occurred; thus, intricate experiences and factors arise.

Complexities within our societal system are another way in which our experiences differ from our co-workers or family members. Understanding that they aren't the same increases the opportunity to understand and be aware of others' experiences rather than reacting to them. It also allows us to look again at how we teach, case manage, police, or supervise when taking these complexities into consideration.

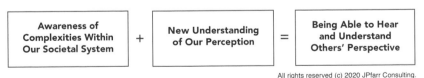

Chapter 3 reviews eleven complexities within the societal system that affect us, our co-workers, and our loved ones. Many more exist. You will find that some complexities are very near and dear to you as you've lived out that complexity your entire life. Other complexities may be new to you, but may be very important to another person's experience. Each complexity could be a book unto itself. This chapter is simply an introduction to the complexities to further increase our knowledge and understanding.

LANGUAGE

Once normalization occurs, language and the use of language will evolve to benefit the normalized group. Consider the right-handed and left-handed example: right-handed is normalized. Language will be used in such a way that associates more positive attributes to the right-handed. For example, if you have an employee who works well for you, he or she may be referred to as your "right-hand man." This is a nod toward two normalized groups: the right-handed and males. If I'm clumsy on the dance floor, someone may refer to me as having "two left feet."

As you look at each triangle set in the last chapter, consider how language often has more asset-based words for the group that is normalized and more deficit-based words for the group that is not normalized. We have historically used derogatory and hurtful names to describe the non-normalized. In response, the non-normalized often used derogatory and hurtful words to describe the normalized. As society has become more conscious of how hurtful language used in this way can be, it has become increasingly unacceptable to use offensive words. Though we still hear some of those insulting names today, it is generally considered ignorant, offensive, and generally less acceptable than in previous generations.

Beyond derogatory names, be aware that when language links positive characteristics with the normalized triangle, it often associates negative characteristics with the downward pointing, non-normalized triangle. Regardless of which triangle we identify with, we may find ourselves using language that way. For example, I am a female, yet I have used the phrase "He throws like a girl!" This statement indicates that a person throws a ball poorly. The message is that throwing "like a boy" is better.

Even though I work on my awareness daily, I still catch myself using phrases in a way that benefit the normalized group. The older I get, the more I catch myself using language that dismisses the younger generation. Once at work while presenting to staff, I asked a teenager if she would please move to another table that wasn't as age-diverse; she kindly agreed. As she was moving, I asked her age. When she responded that she was seventeen, I exclaimed, "Oh child, you are still a baby. So much to learn yet." Later in the presentation when we were talking about language complexity, she pointed out that when I found out her age, I'd called her a baby, assumed she had much to learn, and emphasized her possible limitations as a deficit rather than considering her age and insight from it possibly being an asset. She was exactly right! I had used language to benefit the norm of adulthood.

We may not bother to learn a group's identity at all. We might just use language such as "those people." Not being recognized or using language that lumps everyone together can feel very dismissive.

Becoming aware of how we use language to benefit the normalized can sometimes be overwhelming. We begin to realize just how much we have been affected by the societal system in which we live and that we may be unintentionally perpetuating these complexities. I continue to catch myself using language that is geared toward the norm. On my good days, I'll acknowledge it and immediately adjust. On my bad days, I am frustrated with myself and with the fact that I have to adjust my language to be politically correct.

DISCUSSION

- Think about the triangles from the previous chapter. What are some examples of language we hear or use that are geared toward the normalized? Please do not consider blatantly derogatory words; think instead of the subtle phrases and words we still hear at work or school that have language geared towards the normalized.

- When we become conscious of using language that benefits the norm, then what? How do we change it? Is it difficult to change?

- How does having asset-based or deficit-based language used to describe you or a group to which you belong impact you? How does it change your view of yourself and others?

- Even if we circled a triangle pointing down, we may still use deficit language on the very group we are a part of. What triangle pointing down represents you and your group that you have found yourself using deficit-based words to describe?

MEDIA

The images we view on our TVs, computer screens, or in the movie theaters often reinforce the normalization within our societal system. Lead characters often represent predominantly normalized triangles. Have you ever seen a movie where the lead character represents a minimum of five downward-pointing triangles—where the lead character is a woman with a disabled body, lesbian, Hindi, informally educated, and has a criminal background? More likely, if the lead character reflects several triangles pointing down, the whole movie is about those triangles. A lead character may have one, two, or maybe three downward-pointing triangles, but often not more than that. I love watching TV shows and movies that I grew up with, but when I do, I am astounded by how the normalized triangles are represented in positive and powerful ways. The "bad guys" are consistently people who have many more downward-facing triangles than the "good guys." (Dovidio, n.d.)

Some will say that media (advertisements, TV shows, movies, and so on) simply portray what sells. Does media influence societal norms or do societal norms influence media? For example, Ellen DeGeneres came out as a person who is gay as did her character on her sitcom. She was strongly advised against coming out and was warned that it would end her career because no one would advertise their products with her. Though she didn't work for three years and has continued to deal with threats of boycotts for stances she takes, today Ellen has her own TV talk show and is the spokesperson for several large companies. (Grossman, 2012) Did Ellen's character coming out as gay on the sitcom change society's understanding and acceptance of people who identify as gay? Or was society's understanding and acceptance of people who identify as gay already changing—and the sitcom and other media just reflected that change?

Often the percentage of people who represent the non-normalized triangles are not shown on TV, in the media, and in movies at same percentage as their counterparts—especially not in lead roles. For example, approximately 8.5% of the population are people with disabilities. Are 8.5% of lead characters in TV shows, in movies, and in video games people with disabilities? Or if approximately 5.6% of the population identifies as Asian American, are 5.6% of lead characters in TV shows, movies, and video games Asian Americans?

DISCUSSION

- Think of a favorite television show, movie, or video game. If you landed on earth from another planet and that television, movie, or video game was your only primer about life on earth, what would you glean from it? What would it teach about the normalized and non-normalized groups?
- When non-normalized people are represented in entertainment media, how are they often portrayed? For example, how are women in video games portrayed? In advertisements? In music videos? What effect does this perpetuate in society? What effect might this have on our male and female children?
- How does not having representation in the media impact us, no matter if you are part of the group not being represented or not?
- How can one complexity reinforce another?

ACTIVITY

- Search online for the "Doll Test" video, an experiment in which children are asked to decide which doll is better, a black doll or a white doll. This experiment reflects how the language and media complexities influence us at a young age.
- Do an online search about how women and people of color are portrayed in advertisements and the media. Research data on how it impacts our perceptions of them.
- Look up #thefirsttimeIsawmyself to read how impactful it has been for individuals to see positive examples on TV of people with whom they identified.

- What are your initial reactions to the video clip(s)?
- How do you feel the media's portrayal of women affects both women and men? How do you feel the media's portrayal of people of color affects people who are white and people of color?
- How does the media reinforce normalization? How does that affect you and your organizations?

OVER-RELATING AND UNDER-RELATING

When we work or live with people who clearly represent different triangles than our own, we have to be willing to listen to their perspectives and experiences. Feeling heard is important to human beings. Listening to someone will require that we not over-relate or under-relate. To over-relate is to project your own story, feelings, or understanding onto someone, especially when it's not relevant.

For example, a person who is unemployed vents about the frustration and hardships of being unable to find full-time employment. The listener, who has been gainfully employed for the past 25 years, over-relates when he or she responds by saying, "I totally understand how you feel." Under-relating in that situation might find the person who is gainfully employed replying in a flat affect or offering no verbal response because he feels he has nothing to contribute to the conversation. In either situation, the person who is unemployed may not feel adequately heard.

When we want to have a successful interaction with a person with whom we share few or no triangles, we may become anxious and tend to over-relate with that person. We may use phrases such as "I understand" or "I know how you feel."

I admit to doing this. As my educational level increased and my career advanced, I moved from poverty to middle class and from being informally educated to formally educated. When I was working with staff or clients who were living in poverty or informally educated, I wanted them to know that I felt their struggle. I would say things like "I understand," even when there was no way I could understand. I knew my experience and I understood what it was like to live in poverty and be informally educated 20 years earlier, but I didn't know what living in poverty and being informally educated today was like from their experience.

Over-relating is a very easy thing to do and often well-intentioned, but it can be incredibly demeaning and lead to ineffective encounters. When a person who has a lot of downward-facing triangles is sharing his or her story with someone who knows mostly upward-facing triangles in his or her life, hearing "I understand" can be insulting.

This became very clear when I attended a conference over thirty-five years ago. The speaker was a man whose experience was primarily in the upward-pointing triangles. As he spoke, he continually told his audience he understood what it was like to be them in their jobs. The audience of mostly women began to demonstrate frustrated behavior. Some tuned the speaker out while others made comments to each other about him. The mere fact that he was not conscious of the differences between him and his audience made his speech ineffective. We, in the audience, did not need him to elaborate on the difference between us; we simply needed him not to over-relate to us.

We like to connect with people and sometimes we do it by over-relating. I have found reflective listening to be a very effective way of allowing people to be heard without over-relating or under-relating to that person. When I am talking with someone, I now say things like "I hear you say . . ." or "So for you, this experience has been . . .," rather than "I understand how you feel" or not acknowledging their story. These subtle changes in my response have made my interactions with people much more effective and genuine. Rather than taking my experience of the societal system and projecting it onto others, I honor their stories by listening. Being conscious of my experience allows me to honor another person's experience and create an authentic relationship.

It is equally easy to under-relate with someone. When we walk into a setting where it is clear that we are with people who have the opposite triangles, we may think we have nothing to which we can relate. Therefore, we may feel reserved or that we can contribute nothing in conversation. When we do not engage or contribute to a conversation, it can cause people to feel self-conscious and uncomfortable—not a very effective communication tool. In my work in social services, sometimes new staff would question how they were going to be effective in working with people with whom they had nothing in common. They tended to under-relate with folks they encountered.

If you work with people, there will be moments—or entire days—when the people you work with frustrate you. When frustrated with others, we often lose our capacity to hear about or care about their experiences. We just want them to do what we want them to do. We will under-relate.

We are much more likely to have authentic conversations when we neither over-relate nor under-relate. When professionals held authentic relationships with me, it helped change my life. They were not my friends; they were role models who did not try to over-relate or under-relate as they taught me how work and school operated. They let me talk about my life from my experience while maintaining high expectations of me.

To experience authentic work relationships is an art form that effective teachers, officers, and social workers demonstrate daily. They can show engagement in the conversation by reflecting back what was said and they still might mention some of their experiences. However, they bring forth their experiences as their experiences, not as a way to over-relate or project onto another.

For example, when recently talking with two single moms in my neighborhood, I said, "I hear that it is really stressful for you when you have to juggle going to school, parenting, and working. That sounds exhausting." They both responded with a heartfelt, "Yes, it is." I continued with, "I remember when I was in school, parenting three children, and working; I turned to things like smoking and eating to escape and alleviate some of the stress. Lord knows I couldn't afford a vacation!" One young woman replied, "Maybe that's why I smoke." The other young woman jumped in with, "Yeah, it is exhausting; people don't get what we go through. We are good people, you know." For this woman, my story of my experience was not what she wanted to reflect upon. It was more important for her to process how it felt to be a single mother. For the other woman, my story gave her insight to her current actions.

DISCUSSION

- Think of a time when you have over-related with someone or when someone has over-related with you. What was it like for you? What caused you to over-relate?
- Have there been times when you have under-related with someone or when someone has under-related with you? What was it like for you? What might you do differently?
- What do you think causes us to under-relate?

DIFFERENT GENERATIONS

Look at the circles that you made on your normalization sheet. Pick one of the triangles you circled. Think about a person who would have also circled that triangle, but who is a generation older or younger than you. People from different generations may have a different experience of the same triangle. For example, if you are a woman, think of the experience your great-grandmother had as a woman as compared to your grandmother, your mother, and you. All of you would have circled the female triangle, but all four women would have different experiences of being a female. It is important to acknowledge the similarities as well as the differences within a triangle.

For example, in my own family, we have had family members with disabled bodies and minds across the generations. But their experiences were very different depending on the era in which they were born. One generation ago, those family members with disabilities were sent to live in institutions at a young age. My generation raised their children with disabilities but did not send them to school. The generations after me not only raise their children with disabilities, but the children are integrated into school.

DISCUSSION
- In what ways have you seen other generations experience one of your triangles differently from how you experience it? In what ways are the triangles the same no matter which generation circles them?
- When have you had tension or conflict with someone because of different experiences though you both represent the same triangle?

INDIVIDUAL VERSUS GROUP
One of the benefits of being part of a normalized triangle is that you can represent yourself as an individual. Unfortunately, those in the non-normalized triangle often find themselves

representing an entire group—whether they actually do or not. For example, in my neighborhood, someone who appeared to be an English-speaking, upper-middle-class, formally educated, white, able-bodied male came out of a bar obviously intoxicated and proceeded to stumble down the street. He was in good spirits, smiling, talking loudly to everyone, wildly gesticulating, and unable to walk a straight line. Some on the street who saw him said, "Well, that guy must be having a good day." Later, I saw someone who appeared to be an impoverished, differently-abled male who was also clearly intoxicated. He too was in good spirits, making his way down the street. Except this time I heard people say, "See how those people are. You're poor, but you can always find money for alcohol." The first man was seen simply as an individual who had too much to drink; the second man represented "those people"—entire triangles of people who did not represent the norm.

Likewise, if I talk about having Native American heritage in a meeting, I instantly become the Native American expert. I suddenly represent all Native Americans, as if all Native Americans share the same opinion.

When working with board members on this topic some years ago, a couple of male board members provided great insight into this complexity. They told about a time when their first female board member joined the team. The woman was an extremely hard worker, attended every meeting, volunteered for extra board activities, always did tasks assigned to her, and had insightful comments. The two board members who were male recalled saying after seeing her perform extremely well for a couple months that maybe it wouldn't be so bad to have more women on the board.

At the same time this woman joined the board, so did another person who was male. The new male board member didn't always complete his tasks adequately, missed meetings, often came late, and never signed up for extra board duties. The two board members recalled how they referred to him as "lazy." If the new female board member would have displayed the same characteristics, they likely would have evaluated that women cannot do the job. During the processing of this complexity, the two board members realized that the board member who was female represented all women to them. But the new board member who was a male represented not all men, but just himself as an individual. Thus, they assigned him an individual characteristic like "lazy." He was not a reflection of male ability.

This complexity also affects how we hear and process information. For instance, I attended a community meeting where three people (Joe, Fred, and Bob) representing several normalized triangles debated with each other. Fred was Mexican American. Days later in a meeting with some community members who had also been in attendance, the debate was referenced. One stated, *"Joe sure does have some strong opinions."* The other person followed, *"Yes, he does! But isn't what Fred said extremely interesting? I didn't know that about Mexican American culture. I find Mexican American culture so fascinating."* Fred had not referenced his culture in his remarks. Fred, as an individual, had an idea that he shared that was debated at the meeting. But when others reflected on it, Fred's idea represented not him as an individual, but all Mexican Americans. My fellow community members had heard and interpreted Joe's comments simply as his individual opinion.

DISCUSSION

- Think about a time when you have been asked to speak for an entire group just because you are a member of that group (not because you are an appointed spokesperson). How did you feel representing an entire group? Why do you think this happens to the non-normalized group more than the normalized group?

- When you are aware that people are perceiving you as not just an individual but as a group you are a part of, how does it impact the way you think and act?

- How might you answer a question differently if you were asked as an individual versus being asked as a representative of an entire group?

- Have you ever taken something someone said and repeated it as if it were true for the entire group? What issues can this cause? When, if ever, is this acceptable?

FIRST GENERATION

Some of your triangles will never change. Others—like your economic status—can change. One unique complexity is being the first generation in a specific triangle.

As you recall from the discussion of the previous complexity, if you are part of a non-normalized group, you often represent the entire group to those outside of it. (McIntosh, 1988) When you come from one group and move to another group, you will have to learn nuances, like how to balance representing the group you come from, while at the same time understanding the group that you are entering. Sometimes the very group you come from will begin to reject you as you move into another group. Being rejected by the group you come from can be devastating.

> As I completed the steps of my formal education, the very people who had helped me survive living in poverty—many of whom were informally educated—were now asking, "Who do you think you are? Do you think you're better than us?"

> At the same time, I still used casual English too often and was considered too loud and flamboyant to be successful in a middle-class work environment. Because I had supervisors who had authentic relationships with me and were willing to teach me how life within these new triangles operated, I was eventually able to be effective in a middle-class work environment. However, it took me years to learn how to balance my relationships within the old groups and gain relationships in the new groups. At times, I had to cut ties with some of my friends in order to be successful in my work

and school. This was extremely difficult and painful.
When I cut old ties but could not yet easily relate
to others at work and school, I was very lonely.

DISCUSSION

- In your experience, what have been the consequences of being the first generation to enter a normalized group? How do the groups that you come from react? How does the normalized group react? How did organizations that understood the complexity of being the first generation support you?
- What are the benefits of moving from a non-normalized triangle to a normalized triangle in a lifetime? What barriers exist in moving from a non-normalized group to the normalized group?
- How do you or your organization help support people who have chosen to pursue another triangle?

IMMIGRANT

Many immigrants who move to a new country not only face the challenges that come with adapting to a new nation, but they also may have a change in normalization status. For some, the country they came from normalized their religion, not Christianity. The language they spoke may have been the normalized language in their country, which may not have been English. They may have obtained formal education in their home country, but their certifications may not be recognized in their new land or their inability to speak the language may render it moot. All the benefits a person may have received growing up as part of normalized groups in their homeland may disappear upon entering another country. They may now be considered part of a group that they cannot relate to, i.e., the informally educated after having been formally educated in their homeland. The loss of benefits and identity due to these changes can be bewildering and frustrating.

Consider the situation of two households in my neighborhood. Across the alley lives a family of color. These neighbors are African Americans whose family has lived in the Unites States for many generations. They are informally educated. Their income level is typically below the poverty line. My next-door neighbor would also be considered an African American, though he is an immigrant from Eritrea. He was formally educated in his homeland where his family was considered middle class. Fleeing Eritrea because of war then finding his professional certifications not recognized in the United States, his class and education status have been disrupted. Though he considers himself an educated middle-class man, this next-door neighbor is now considered informally educated and underclass in the eyes of the societal system. When he immigrated to the United States, he switched from several normalized to non-normalized triangles and lost the benefits of belonging to the normalized groups.

Though these two families have had very different experiences of the societal system, they are often seen as part of the same groups: informally educated, lower class, and of color — both having African heritage. Both identify as people of color, but not necessarily with each other. When I speak with my neighbor who immigrated fifteen years ago, he has frequently made statements reflecting that he does not consider himself to be like the generational African Americans across the alley.

DISCUSSION
- Have you or could you imagine moving to a new country and realizing the very identities you grew up with are no

longer the identities the societal system assigns to you? How would you handle this? What support would be helpful?

- Have you ever been associated with a group that you did not feel you were a part of that did not represent who you were? How did you respond to that association?
- How would you explain friction between a group of people immigrating into a new societal system with those whose ancestors lived out that immigration pattern several generations ago? What are possible supports that could help bring more awareness and alleviate some of the friction?

THE ONE-PICTURE PHENOMENON

Sometimes we unintentionally put the normalized triangles together to assume one picture, a depiction that may not be accurate. For example, we normalize middle class, employed, white, and formally educated. When we encounter people who are formally educated and white, we may assume they are also employed and middle class before having any proof.

The same is true regarding downward-pointing triangles. For example, disabled, lower and poverty class, informally educated, and unemployed are all non-normalized groups. When we encounter a person who is living with a disability and informally educated, we may assume she is also underclass and/or unemployed.

For example, a friend of mine has a disease that has attacked her body, leaving her with only a limited ability to control her hand. She uses an electric wheelchair operated with a stick hand control. Her speech is very limited. When she attends fundraisers, people often assume she is a person representing the clientele for whom the funds are being raised. Formally educated and wealthy, she attends fundraisers as a major donor, but rarely is she initially perceived that way. She observes how people change their perception of her as they learn where she lives (a well-known wealthy area) and where she went to school (an Ivy League education). She has noted that as her body changed, assumptions about her education level, economic status, and other identities changed as well.

DISCUSSION
- How can you check yourself when you are making assumptions about people?
- How do you feel when someone makes assumptions about you and your identity?
- What are some triggers for assumptions we make quickly?

INTERSECTIONALITY

Every triangle we circled impacts the next triangle we circled and vice versa. Our experiences of any given circled triangle intersect with the next. These intersections can lead two people with one shared identity (i.e., female) to experience the same identity very differently because of other differing triangles circled (i.e., of color, underclass).

> I am a cisgender female who also identifies as Native American. When I gather with female friends, we often discuss frustration at issues such as unequal pay between men and women. Once at a meeting of women who were primarily upper-middle class, white, formally educated, and of European heritage, I stated, "I just want us to stop disappearing!" They all agreed and spoke about how invisible they could feel at work around male colleagues. And I clarified that I meant it literally: Native American women actually disappear and

often little is done to ascertain what happened to them. (Lucchesi, PhD & Echo-Hawk, 2018) The other women had no idea this was happening, that is was not hyperbole.

As stated previously, it is not about anyone in the group having a "right" or "better" viewpoint. It is about realizing that though we may have commonality because some of our identities are the same, we may also have different experiences and opinions based on other triangles we circled.

DISCUSSION

- Which triangles did you circle that sometimes give you a different viewpoint than another person with a similar identity? Which triangles tend to dominate over categories, regardless of being normalized or non-normalized?
- If you are a person of color who is upper-class, formally educated, non-disabled, and employed, how would or wouldn't that shape your viewpoint from a person of color who is impoverished, informally educated, disabled, and unemployed?
- How do we ensure we are able to hear about people's different experiences even when they hold some of the same identities as us?

YOU ARE AFFECTED BY NORMALIZATION

No matter where or how you grew up, you are affected by normalization. People who grew up in a very homogenized setting sometimes argue that the effects of normalization didn't impact them, but no experience excludes normalization because every one of us has a unique experience of the societal system.

My grandmother was a Native American who lived on a reservation. I have blue eyes and latte-colored skin. I lived both in predominantly white, rural small towns and Native American reservations. If normalization did not exist, if it had not affected me and others in the community, then my experience in the white and Native American communities would have been similar. But because normalization exists—because we are all affected by it—I was treated in two very different ways in the two communities. In the reservation communities, even though my grandmother and mother are Native, I was often called a derogatory word for white person. When living in the predominantly white community, I didn't always relate to or view things the way others did. My experience in these two communities still impacts me today.

DISCUSSION

- How has normalization affected you?
- How do we continue to perpetuate normalization?
- How can different aspects of normalization affect our life experiences?

INTERNALIZATION

Living in a societal system that normalizes different groups gives us each a different experience. Language and the media around us reflect the normalization that has occurred in our societal system. Each of us is given messages, directly and indirectly, about who we are, based on the groups we represent and messages we internalize to varying degrees. Internalization is the integration into one's own identity or a sense of self of the attitudes and messages that the societal system sends.

Review the triangles you circled. What messages, attitudes, or opinions have you received because you represent that triangle, either positive or negative? Though we like to say that sticks and stones may break our bones, but words will never hurt us, the messages we receive can negatively and positively affect how we view ourselves and others.

By the time I was thirty years old, I had risen out of poverty, was employed by the local county welfare department, and had a regular, substantial income. Wanting to get new furniture and carpeting for the house I purchased, I went to a bank for a loan and filled out the application. Everything was approved except I was informed that I had to have my husband cosign for the loan. Why would my husband have to cosign for a loan? It wasn't his house or money!

Unbeknownst to me, at that time women could not secure loans on their own![4] They had to be cosigned by a parent or husband, even when the woman had adequate income. This infuriated me; my husband was not in the picture and was, frankly, a detriment. I appealed the process, wrote letters, and called up a friend from the newspaper to complain. Ultimately, the bank changed the policy. It was one of the first times I consciously and actively fought against the message of who I was supposed to be as a woman.

When I reflect on that experience today, I wonder if I would have thought to complain if that incident had happened while I was still living in poverty *and had not yet obtained some formal education. Sometimes when you are not part of the normalized triangle, you are sent the message that your voice does not matter at all or as much. You internalize that message and wonder why you would exert the energy to complain if it would go nowhere.*

Over the years, I have been sent both positive and negative messages because I'm a female. I have internalized both and acted on both. Being female in a societal system that normalizes males has had ramifications on my life, just as being male in a societal system that normalizes males has ramifications on men's lives.

I've always immensely appreciated the fact that I am a woman, though I had a rocky start. I happen to be endowed with a knock-down, drag-out figure, with large breasts and big hips. In my youth, I was bullied by boys but also—and more cruelly—by women. There was a prejudice about how I was built. My father's friends felt that they could make rude or disrespectful comments about me simply because I had that kind of figure. It was very confusing and hurtful with the lasting effect of making me suspicious of interactions with men. These older men sent a distinct message. I internalized it and projected it onto other men. I learned to expect disrespectful comments from men, but I was always surprised when other women judged me and made rude comments about me before getting to know me. They too were sent messages about women and they too internalized those messages; it affected how they viewed me. I could understand why someone from another triangle would view me in a certain way, but negative assumptions coming from the triangle I represented was perplexing and painful.

This internalization has also played out in my professional world. As my career advanced, I sat on several boards that were equally mixed with men and women. During a meeting, I often noted that when a woman brought up an idea, no one would acknowledge it—not even the other women. Later in the meeting, if a man presented the same idea, it was often the women who responded with positive comments toward his "insightful" idea.

When I supervised a large staff, I observed how the male staff often asked for a higher salary than what was posted or they asked for additional benefits. Their female counterparts would rarely ask for a higher salary, and if they did, it was usually without the confidence that their male co-workers had and with a lot of attempts at justifying why they should receive the additional money or benefit. (Bussey, 2014; Ludden, 2011)

Every circle we made on the triangle chart affects our identities. The societal system sends messages, directly and indirectly, to everyone within it. We internalize and act on them in varying degrees, consciously or unconsciously. The more we are aware of this complexity, the more we become conscious of the messages we receive, how we internalize them, and how we choose to act on them, if at all.

DISCUSSION

- As you look at the triangles you circled, what messages do you think you have been sent directly and indirectly about your inclusion in that group? How have you internalized these messages? How have you acted on them?
- Challenge yourself to think about messages you have sent others that reflect your assumptions about which groups they are in. What comes to mind?
- How does normalization and the complexities found within a societal system that normalizes certain groups impact the way we view each other? How does it impact the work we do?
- Visit the website run by Harvard University called Project Implicit and take the "implicit association test" (IAT), a rapid-response task which measures how easily you can pair items from different categories. Are you surprised by your results?
- How can we move beyond these societal constructs and interact with people for who they are and not the triangles they hold? How would our organizations be different if we moved toward doing that?

HOMEWORK

- For the next week, take the first five complexities and intentionally look for them within your interactions and observations. Where do you see them play out? Now that you have awareness, how can you respond differently?
- On the second week, take the last six complexities and again intentionally look for them. Where do you see them play out? How did you respond?

CHAPTER 4

P O S S I B I L I T Y

KEYS TO UNLOCK INDIVIDUAL, ORGANIZATION, AND
COMMUNITY POTENTIAL TO MAXIMIZE OUR
AWARENESS

As we gain a greater sense of understanding (being aware of where
we are part of the norm and where we are not) and process our
experience with the complexities found within a societal system,
we can move toward action.

INDIVIDUAL KEYS

First, we want to take action to continue to foster awareness. We
must be willing to watch and listen for how normalization and
complexities are all around us and how they impact our individual
interactions. This awareness will allow us to respond in a way that
is not reactionary and does not perpetuate normalization. Rather,
we can choose to respond in a way that allows others to feel heard
and for us to ultimately be more effective.

For example, if you have ever loved a child (yours, a niece, nephew,
or godchild), haven't you wanted "better" for that child? Most of
us have over-extended ourselves to get something "better" for the
child we love. I was once at a wealthy function waiting for the valet

to return my car when my dream car drove up. As a young driver exited her car, I complimented her on it. I have always wanted this particular car, but with a $100,000 price tag, it remains a fantasy. We had a short conversation about the car in which she stated, "My mom and dad got it for me for my sixteenth birthday!"

Earlier in my life, I would have immediately judged her and her parents then acted out of my negative judgements when interacting with them. Now, I don't begrudge her that car; her parents are obviously circling the wealthy triangle that allows them to obtain an expensive car for their daughter. I don't know if they are fabulously wealthy or if they are working three jobs to lease it. Similarly, I do not begrudge parents in middle-or working-class households who want their child to experience a theme-park vacation (though they are financially stretched to afford it) who charge the whole thing on credit cards.

If you have circled triangles like underclass, you may not have $100,000 to buy your child a new car or access to a line of credit to finance a big vacation. Still, you may be able to buy the newest shoes, jeans, or purse, even if they are knock-offs from the back of the van that drives through my neighborhood.

Taking time to become more conscious of our experiences allows us to be more open to how others may experience our societal system. This understanding invites us not to react out of judgement, but allows us the ability to hold a new understanding where we can listen and be most effective in our interactions with others.

Take this awareness and bring it to the work or volunteering you do. In places where you find yourself judging another's actions or responses, take a step back and consider how your triangles are impacting how you view the situation. Take another step back to consider if the person you are currently reacting to may have had a different experience of the societal system.

Throughout my social service career, I would see staff who were part of several normalized groups judge a patron who was identified with many non-normalized groups. When the patron came in with her nails and hair done carrying a name-brand purse then would argue about why she had to pay a $5 co-pay, staff would typically react with complaints like, "How is she going to have her hair and nails done, buy a name-brand purse, but argue with me about a $5 co-pay?" When staff and I would process the situation, they often did not know that many people in impoverished and underclass neighborhoods sometimes barter to get their nails and hair done. And even if they paid a nail salon, that is one way to take a break and do something to pamper yourself. I would ask staff to consider what they have done to take a break for themselves. Much of what they mentioned was not attainable when you don't have the transportation or funds that middle and upper-middle class affords you.

The effects of those judgements and the experience of often finding yourself in the non-normalized group don't just evaporate. Once we have more awareness of how normalization impacts our perception and interactions, we can explore how we hold those experiences within our body. Though this book does not address that issue specifically, I lift up for further reading *My Grandmother's Hands: Racialized Trauma and the Pathway to Mending Our Hearts and Bodies* by therapist Resmaa Menakem (Central Recovery Press, 2017). In this excellent book, the author works through research and understanding of the effects of historical trauma on white and black bodies.

Another way we can move beyond labels within our societal system is to not make assumptions about which triangles people are in. When we engage in conversation with people who may have little in common with us, allow each person to inform us of who he or she is and what their identities mean to them. Ultimately, we want to move beyond the identities that come with normalization.

In return, whenever possible, don't use the identities in the triangle chart to describe people if it is not necessary. My neighborhood is very diverse and I often hear people informing me of what other people's identities are (or at least how they perceive them to be) when it has no relevance to the story. For example, a neighbor said to me, "Oh, you know Bob. He lives one block over and he's gay. He stopped by my house to see if I wanted flowers." Often when we apply labels, it is when people represent a non-normalized triangle. I have never heard someone say, "Bob, the straight man who lives one block over stopped by to see if I wanted flowers."

These actions help us stop unconsciously perpetuating a societal system that normalizes certain traits while opening opportunity to get to know someone as they wish to be identified.

DISCUSSION

- Think of situations where you may have judged or reacted to someone at work. When you bring the awareness differences between your experiences, how can it help bridge understanding?
- At a party or social gathering, how often do you ask a person about which triangle he or she identifies with? How do his or her answers impact the way that person is viewed and engaged with from that point on?

- How can these actions perpetuate normalization? What conversation starters could be used instead? (I.e., "What's good in your life right now?")
- How do you think we hold the experiences of normalization and non-normalization within our bodies? What might the cumulative physical and mental effect of long-term non-normalized experiences be?

ORGANIZATIONAL KEYS
FORMULA FOR EFFECTIVE CHANGE

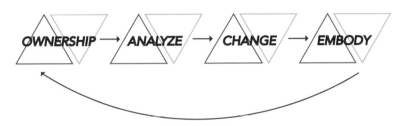

With our new insights, let's analyze how we have done business and consider what we want to change. Often, it is not enough to decide to make a change; we must also be intentional about how we are going to support the changes we make.

Know that management and those who hold more normalized identities will often rate the organization higher than those working on the front line or those who relate to identities which are not part of the normalized.

Begin by rating your organization on the chart below.

Stage 1: The Exclusionary Organization	Stage 2: "The Stage"	Stage 3: The Compliance Organizations
Openly operates out of the normalized triangles experiences Intentionally does not work with one or more identities belonging to the group that is not normalized DESIGNED TO MAINTAIN THAT THE NORMALIZED GROUPS WILL REMAIN IN POSITIONS OF POWER within the organization	The policies of who the organization works with and hires have expanded to include all identities in the triangle chart yet the overall operations and culture are very similar to thirty and fifty years ago Though there is some diversity most of the leadership and positions of power are held by predominantly normalized dominant people There is acknowledgement of the all identities and even an attempt to understand all views but operations and change in culture has not occurred	An organization who is committed to learning about and removing the obstacles that are inherent in the Club organization. Will have diversity trainings for staff Will try to intentionally hire groups who historically may not have had access Will provide some access to some members of groups who are not part of the normalized More knowledge and action then in the Club but still operates in a way that is more geared towards those who are part of the normalized group. Thus, often does not maintain employees who represent identities of groups that are not normalized. And/or outcomes with customers is not as successful with people representing groups that are not normalized

An adaptation of the
Multicultural Organization Development (MCOD) Stage Model

SOURCES: Jackson, B. W (2006). Theory and practice of multicultural organization development. In Jones, B. B. & Brazzel, M. (Eds.), The NTL Handbook of organization Development and Change (pps. 139-154). San Francisco, CA: Pfeiffer. Jackson, B. W., & Hardiman, R. (1994). Multicultural organization development. In E.Y. Cross, J.H. Katz, F.A. Miller, & E. W. Seashore (Eds.), The promise of diversity: Over 40 voices discuss strategies for eliminating discrimination in organizations (pp. 231-239). Arlington, VA: NTL Institute.

Stage 4: The Affirming Organizations	Stage 5: The Redefining Organizations	Stage 6: The Multicultural Organizations
An organization who has removed numerous obstacles found in the previous stages thus operates in significantly different way then ever before	Continues to work to ensure full inclusion of members is felt by all identities	Mission, values, operations, services and outcomes reflect the contributions and interested of the identities found on the triangle chart.
Actively and effectively recruits and promotes all identities found in the triangle chart especially those who have historically been denied access	Actively completes Organizational analysis that allows all voices to be heard and acted on	Have closed any achievement gaps found in the previous stages
Conducts trainings that lead to action and change of operation	The organization has such a new awareness and has been affirming for so long that the organization itself has to change	
Begin to see many more identities from groups that are not normalized at ALL levels, especial positions of power		
Hire diverse identities and maintain their employment at the same rates		
Begin to close any achievement gaps that previously existed in outcomes		

DISCUSSION

- Explain how you came up with your rating for your organization.
- How do you think other people from your organization might rate the organization differently?
- What can you and your organization do to intentionally move up to the next ranking?

Once you have rated your organization and had a discussion about it, you may be ready for action. The below key can be used for an individual or for an entire organization.

How does this individual action and/or organizational policy benefit the normalized group (for example, middle class)?

How does this individual action and/or organizational policy create an obstacle for those who are not part of the normalized group (for example, poverty)?

What individual action and/or organizational policy can we change to ensure that all benefit?

How do we— as individuals, an institution, and a community— support this change?

If you use this tool to assess your organization, begin by asking which outcomes you currently have that you are not satisfied with. For example, when working recently with an entire organization's staff, they discussed how they were not satisfied with their client retention rate. The organization had recently sponsored a 16-week course for women who were single, had children, and earned a low income; the retention for the course was low. When they discussed why the rate was low, the staff gave several individual-lens and societal-system-lens answers. The staff spoke about how when you live in poverty, you have a higher chance of unreliable transportation, how daycare is an issue, and how the women they work with are often exhausted so may not want to attend class. They also talked about how things come up; watching your sister's kids or helping out a cousin would be more of a priority for the women than attending class.

All of these points were valid. But none of them came from the institutional lens. True, the societal system may be set up to hinder transportation for people who earn a lower income and yes, as individuals, people earning a lower income may feel that assisting a relationship with a need is more important than attending a class, but what role does the institution play in the current low retention rate?

Remember that a system is perfectly designed to get the results it is getting. With this in mind, I asked the staff to reflect on what role the institution had in a low retention rate. The staff (who had all been through this training) mentioned the clear difference between staff and the course participants. The participants tended to represent more non-normalized identities from the triangles pointing down than the staff did.

One staff member said, "We are primarily middle to upper-middle class, formally educated, employed, documented, mostly white, able-bodied, and able-minded women! The women in the program do not have the benefits of all those triangles. I think we created a program from our experience, not from theirs, and I don't think it is as effective as it could be."

After a long conversation with the entire staff, there was a consensus that if the staff represented more of the triangles (both the normalized and those who are not part of the normalized), the program they would create would be more effective, thus increasing the retention rate. At this point, I asked the HR director to get the hiring policies for the institution and asked everyone to look at these four questions.

The staff felt that if the organization' employees would reflect a more diverse experience among the normalized and non-normalized, then we would have to explore the hiring policies. How is it that those who got hired were from so many of the same experiences? How did the institution and the hiring policies contribute to this? If we could understand this, we could discuss the changes that might need to be made and how to support those changes in an attempt to have a more diverse staff. A more diverse staff could create a more effective 16-week program and thus increase retention rates.

The staff simply began to take each hiring policy through the four questions found in Tool #1.

DISCUSSION
The first policy stated that the application process was now online only. The human resource director clarified they had made the switch from paper to electronic-only application a few years ago.

Explore this policy—to have all applications completed online only—through the four questions:

- How does this institutional policy benefit the normalized group (for example, middle class)?
- How does this institutional policy create an obstacle for those who are not part of the normalized group (for example, people living in poverty)?
- What institutional policy can we change to ensure that all benefit? How can we change it?

- How do we—as individuals, an institution, and a community—support this change?

The staff realized that the majority of the middle and upper economic classes had computer and internet access as well as knowledge and experience applying online. Completing an application online would be as simple as turning on the computer in your home.

Addressing the second question in this key, the staff listed the numerous obstacles a person earning a lower income might have completing the same task. People earning a low income are less likely to have computers in the home. Completing an online application would thus require leaving one's home. Another staffer mentioned that in his experience, people earning a low income typically have less reliable transportation and less reliable daycare. Having to go outside of the home to complete an online application might require a favor from a friend to give you a ride and a favor from another friend to provide daycare for your child. Other potential obstacles surfaced such as limited hours at the library or a line for the computer at the community center.

As the staff moved to the third question, many solutions were discussed, including going back to paper, doing nothing differently, or offering both paper and online applications. The pros and cons to all the solutions were discussed.

The staff agreed that because all jobs required the knowledge and ability to use a computer, they would not go back to paper applications. They would address barriers to completing an online application by converting a large storage area into a comfortable workstation with two functioning computers and an area for kids to play. They would keep it open 24-hours a day with no time limits on the computers.

Creating change brings an opportunity to receive new outcomes, but intentionally supporting change allows for a shift in the institutional culture. One policy change does not by itself shift the culture or attitude of an institution. Individuals within the institutions have to support the change to sustain it and to make lasting shifts in institutional operation and culture. Without answering the last question found in the first key, this institution could make their planned changes and then within months likely have "Out of Order" signs taped to the computers or staff not informing applicants that this resource room even exists. For change to be impactful, there must be a plan on how the change will be sustained.

When answering question from the fourth key (how to support the change), the IT director put in her budget to purchase, set up, and maintain the computers. The facilities manager put in his work orders to paint the room and get it ready for internet access. A staff member said she would work with her local religious organization to donate children's books and toys for the children's area. Another staffer said an organization she was a part of had beautiful art that she would get to put on the wall. The front desk staff said that the vast majority of people who wanted a paper application stopped there for it, so they would train all reception staff to ensure that anyone who came in for a paper application would be informed about the room. They also would ensure the room was cleaned daily.

DISCUSSION

After this discussion about the first policy, the staff returned to the hiring policies to examine the second policy through the lens of the four keys. This time, the policy was regarding how applications were graded. The institution deducted points for grammatical errors on the application.

- How does this individual action and/or institutional policy benefit the normalized group (for example, middle class)?
- How does this individual action and/or institutional policy create an obstacle for those who are not part of the normalized group (for example, living in poverty)?
- What individual action or institutional/community policy can we change to ensure that all benefit?
- How do we as individuals, an institution, and a community support this change?

The staff had another passionate discussion. In the end, they felt that the deduction was credible and would stay in place for jobs where grammar was crucial to the job duties, such as grant writers and development. For front desk and case manager positions, they would no longer deduct points based on grammar. Those departments felt that being able to build relationships was a much more important skill set than writing notes that were grammatically correct.

As you reflect on this activity, keep in mind that change can bring many different reactions from people. Some love change and embrace it. Others fear it or ignore it. Some react passive-aggressively out of anxiety in the face of change. Be aware of normal human emotions around change to ensure a space where people can process their thoughts and feelings.

It was after completing the second policy that a staff member threw up his hands and said, "Well, hey, everybody. Come work for us! We don't care if you can spell or turn on a computer. If you're warm, we'll hire you." Understanding that change can trigger an emotional response, the staff and I asked him to keep talking to help us understand the source of his frustration. After a few minutes, he articulated what everyone understood. "It seems to me we are lowering the expectations."

The staff had a great discussion on this topic. Were they lowering expectations or creating another path so all could meet an existing expectation? There is a subtle difference.

Becoming conscious of our experience allows us to see the advantages and limitations we have. To move forward by intentionally ensuring that everyone can have access and advantages is honorable, but the soft bigotry of low expectations is always a possibility as we make change. The staff concluded that they were not lowering expectations with the changes they made regarding the first policy. Regarding the second policy change, they felt that not deducting for incorrect grammar was not lowering the expectation; it was allowing people to have access to jobs where grammar was not the primary role. They believed that as an institution, they should continue to create a path where employees could enhance their writing skills. The institution created a partnership with a local community college allowing current employees to attend up to three classes at no cost if the class was related to work or improving English skills. The staff felt that if everyone had access to this, then the policy regarding deduction for incorrect grammar could stand for management level positions as these jobs required skilled writing.

DISCUSSION
- Give examples of how you as an individual could use these keys in your interactions.
- How could an organization you are associated with use these keys?

We live in a societal system that normalizes one group over the other. Our understanding and awareness of this allows us to identify the complexities that arise in a social system. This awareness can allow us to better understand our family members, co-workers, and others who may experience the societal system very differently than we do.

COMMUNITY KEY

Five Step Process to Successful Community Efforts

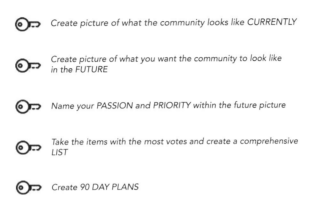

Create picture of what the community looks like CURRENTLY

Create picture of what you want the community to look like in the FUTURE

Name your PASSION and PRIORITY within the future picture

Take the items with the most votes and create a comprehensive LIST

Create 90 DAY PLANS

Now that we have a deeper, individual awareness of normalization issues and are more open to hearing each other's experiences, we can bring together the many different identities that exist in our community to think about what we want to achieve. The strongest community action happens when we have many identities at the table. The five-step process that follows can serve as a framework to work toward a common goal. This process works best with an outside, detached facilitator.

Step 1: When we come together, we begin by talking about what life looks like now. As you discuss the current realities within your community, you may have conflicting viewpoints; that is expected. If we hold different identities and experiences within our community, then at times we will naturally have differing views of the current reality. All viewpoints should be honored and recorded.

Step 2: Once we have a picture of what our community currently looks like, we are ready to envision the future we want. Imagine your community in 5-7 years as a model of health and happiness. What would be going on? If other people were visiting your community to replicate what you have created, what would they see, hear, and feel? Write down specific goals that would create a new paradigm for your community.

It is worth noting that as you complete the future story, someone will invariably "Yes, but…" an idea. When we respond to ideas with comments like, "Yes, of course we want more walking paths, but we don't have a budget for it," we have unintentionally brought us back to what life looks like now. It should be noted that the *current* picture is very powerful because we see it, live in it, and have to deal with it. The future story is still abstract, something we can only imagine. But the future is an important investment. We've all attended brainstorming sessions where the only goal was to dream about what could be when someone says, "Yes, but…" and pops the thought bubbles with new, innovative ideas. Without a goal to reach, there is little likelihood of a concrete plan being formed to attain it. On this step, don't allow the limitations of today dictate your tomorrow.

Step 3: Once the community has created a future story, everyone present gets to vote on two things in the future picture: one vote for an idea that they have passion for and another vote for what they feel is a priority. Sometimes our passions and priorities are different. I may be passionate about new walking paths, but I think it is a priority that we increase job opportunities in our community. Once everyone has voted, tally it up. Take the top three to five topics that received the most votes. Divide participants into those three to five groups so people who are interested on working on walking paths will meet together. Those who want more job opportunities will meet in another space.

Step 4: In small groups formed around a common goal, invite participants to create a comprehensive list of all the things that have to occur to accomplish their future goal.

Step 5: From this list of requirements for achieving the future goal, create a 90-day plan with tangible steps. When you complete the 90-day plan, ensure that the work load is evenly distributed. No one should leave feeling overwhelmed by the process. Likewise, no one should be excluded.

Once the 90-day plans are complete, the community has a road map from where they are starting, where they want to go, and a concrete plan of actions that will move them down the road. Agree to come together every ninety days to report on progress, support each other, and create a new 90-day plan as needed.

90-Day Plan

IDEA *(WHAT IS GOING TO BE ACCOMPLISHED)*			
INTENT *(WHY)*			
IMPLEMENTATION STEPS *(HOW)*	WHO	WHEN	WHERE
1.	1.	1.	1.
2.	2.	2.	2.
3.	3.	3.	3.
4.	4.	4.	4.
5.	5.	5.	5.
6.	6.	6.	6.
7.	7.	7.	7.
8.	8.	8.	8.
9.	9.	9.	9.
10.	10.	10.	10.
Coordinator			
Team Members			
Start Date			
End Date			

DISCUSSION

- How can your community use this five-step process?
- This process can be used within an organization. What benefits and outcomes could you envision your organization gaining by completing this process?
- This process can be utilized on an individual basis. In what situations would this be helpful when working one-on-one? How would you implement it for an individual?

HOMEWORK

Take the key learning that was most meaningful to you and implement it at work, in your community, individually, or with another person.

IN CLOSING

You and I live within a Societal System that inherently places identities upon us—male or female, white or black, and so on. Whether these labels are accurate or needed is not the point of this book. Instead, we have addressed the fact that these identities exist and inform our understanding of ourselves and others. We also acknowledge that our societal system normalizes some identities over others, which leads to people experiencing the societal system in vastly different ways.

To successfully engage in the societal system, we must understand how the identities placed upon us have impacted our experiences and how those experiences can universally affect our perceptions, especially of self and others. Not understanding how experiences and perceptions affect engagement in society perpetuates a system where our fellow humans do not have the same access and voice within the societal system. But understanding these varying experiences and their effects can help us on every level of engagement—in our work and worship, our communities and institutions, and even within our families.

In today's polarized world, there is an urgency to our awareness! Equipped with a new understanding and practical tools to examine individual, organizational, and community practices, together we can move beyond the identities that society places upon us in ways that benefit everyone.

With new awareness, insight, and action, our policies, organizations, communities—and our world—can be transformed.

SUGGESTIONS FOR FACILITATORS

Thank you for your leadership as a facilitator. One of the most difficult tasks of facilitating is to create a safe place where varied experiences can be shared and heard without judgement. This is no small task, but it can create a life-changing experience for participants.

When forming study groups, keep in mind that the more diversity (of age, gender, religion, cultural background, physical ability, etc.) represented, the more impact the discussion will likely have. Gaining a deeper awareness of the world we live in and the people we interact with will allow us to maximize our personal and professional effectiveness. There's no better way to achieve this than to create discussion groups composed of people with a variety of experiences and viewpoints.

A facilitator's primary role is to ensure that each participant is listened to and that the group remains a safe place for each person to reflect upon his or her experience. Facilitators will find it helpful to have previous experience or training in group work, as well as skills in reflective listening and maintaining group boundaries.

Please ensure that you read the book in its entirety and work through the questions and homework before facilitating a group. Not only will you be more prepared, but you will have processed your own experiences before leading others in processing theirs. As you know (if you're a trained facilitator), facilitating a group discussion of the book is not the same as teaching the material within it. Each participant will have his or her own understanding of the material to share with the larger group. As a facilitator, you may spend your time modeling how to listen and ensuring people feel safe and heard.

This book will address the identities (displayed in triangle illustrations) that we have been told, directly or indirectly, that we belong to. Often the categories we represent impact how we experience and see the world. Some of us hold deep pride in some of the categories we represent; they may have brought us great joy or great pain. Facilitators should be aware that delving into this material may be emotional for participants. Maintain a safe place where people can express their emotions. Ensure that the group remains a caring place for people to process their experiences and feelings. Help group members learn how to listen to each other and resist being defensive when hearing others' stories.

GENERAL FACILITATOR NOTES

For facilitators who use this in the workplace, within a religious setting, for a book club, or with students, please consider the following:

- At or before the first meeting, decide expectations regarding preparation and reading. Will participants read the entire book (not recommended) before you start or a chapter at a time before each session? There has been a lot of success with groups getting together for an hour over a meal to get to know each other, set up guidelines, and receive the book. Then the group reads chapters 1 and 2 before the second session. Schedule a 2–2.5-hour second session to reflect on those two chapters. (Sometimes groups need a second session for chapters 1 and 2.) Repeat for chapter 3 and again for chapter 4. Alternatives might include reading and debriefing one chapter at a time.

- Ensure comfortable, circular seating to encourage discussion, preferably around a table for a kitchen-conversation feel. A comfortable and accessible setting for all is very important.

- Consider meeting over a meal or provide snacks and beverages. The more comfortable the environment, the more relaxed participants will be.

- Open with informal introductions that encourage participants to get to know one another and an ice-breaker to increase their comfort levels. Ice-breaker ideas include having individuals share with the group a picture on their cellphones of something or someone that is important to them (including, of course, only appropriate photos and those participants are comfortable sharing).

- Ensure that every participant has a book.

GOALS & FACILITATOR TIPS BY CHAPTER

Chapter 1
- Ensure each participant comprehends systemic thinking—looking at the societal system as a whole—and that societal system normalizes one thing over the other. This is not about right or wrong or good versus bad, but helps explain why people have different experiences within the same system.

Chapter 2
- This chapter's goals are acknowledgement of the different normalized identities, realization of what identities we hold personally, and an openness to hear how this may impact our perception.
- You may also have to help participants not obsess on the identities and definitions. As we get nervous or feel anxiety, it is often easier to move out of our bodies and into our heads. We over-analyze information rather than absorb it.
- As stated, we are very aware that we are condensing very large topics and identities into a triangle chart. We acknowledge this and ask for understanding. If any participant whose identity IS that of a triangle pointing down, one that is not normalized, AND he/she feels it does not accurately describe him/her, the person may add his/her preferred identity on his/her chart. This should NOT be true for the identities for the normalized group. To be a part of the normalized group where most know your identity and still wanting it changed is a privilege. Being part of a group which is not normalized—where folks often do not know or acknowledge your identity—and wanting to be identified accurately is essential to the task at hand.

- If needed, help people process which triangle they should circle. Be careful never to inform people what their identity is or tell them what to circle based on your assumptions.
- Encourage people to circle all or at least some of the normalized triangle if they receive benefits from the societal system for having all or some of that identity. Once a male (male-looking and gender-identifying as male) participant did not want to circle the male triangle because he was a passionate feminist. We thanked him for his passion and understanding and reminded him the first step to assisting another group is by acknowledging the benefits you hold. Just because one is not comfortable receiving the benefits of a normalized triangle does not mean they should not circle that triangle.
- For some participants who are people of color passing as white (typically of visually ambiguous ethnic heritage), they may choose to circle half of the triangle with the identity of white and half the triangle with the identity of color to honor both parents. Or they may circle the triangle identity white to honor that they get the benefits of being white passing and then circle the triangle representing a heritage not being European.
- Sometimes media and literature talk about triangle sets together that we have separated. For example, we have the anatomical sex you were born (M/F, I) as one set, the way you express yourself sexually (Heterosexual/LGBPQA) as another set, and the gender with which you identify (Cisgender/T, GN, GF, GD, GNB) as yet another set. This is to help articulate that these represent three very different topics though often sexual expression and gender are culturally grouped together.
- Acknowledge that when your experience and identity are not part of the normalized, groups can gain power and voice

within the societal system by joining efforts. Nevertheless, for this exercise, we honor each group independently.

- Another example of parsing out groups that are often culturally lumped together could be the color of one's skin and physical attributes. White/of color is one set of triangles and the ethnicity with which you identify (European-based/non-European based; example, Native American) is a separate set of triangles. This allows us to begin to see the complexities within a societal system that normalizes different things. For example, you may receive the benefits of being perceived as white (especially by people who identify as white) and have physical features of your European ancestors. But you may also identify as having a Native American ethnicity. These two triangle sets allow you to honor your Native American identity (not normalized), but also acknowledges the benefits you get from having dominant European physical features (normalized). Other relatives who inherited dominant Native American physical features (including the non-normalized darker skin color) may have experienced being treated differently because of their skin tone. You can both be proud of your native ancestry but recognize you may have had different experiences due to appearance.
- Separating some of the topics and identities that are sometimes put together in our societal system will help us better understand the complexities that arise within the societal system in later chapters.

Chapter 3

- Complexities do exist. As stated, each complexity could be a book by itself. We are simply trying to get participants to see that complexities exist and they impact our experiences, which in turn directly impact how we perceive things.

- We strongly suggest that you read other sources on any complexity that is new to you or just not as meaningful.
- Begin to have participants think about how these complexities impact the work they do and how their organization could address them. For example, many organizations want participants to achieve different goals: get your GED, show up for appointments on time, eat healthier, etc. This may result in someone's identity changing to a normalized (formal education) triangle. Once we understand the first-generation complexity exists, how might it change how we separate people on their journeys of achievement?

Chapter 4

- Process how the previous chapter impacts how we perceive situations and be open to how others may look at it. There are then very concrete tools that individuals, organizations, and communities can use.
- Ensure the participants comprehend the tool and feel equipped to utilize the 90-day plan.
- Have a concrete way to end the sessions. Maybe have participants speak about one thing they became aware of and how it will impact how they do their work or use it in their personal lives.
- Allow for an opportunity for participants to thank each other for being willing to share and learn from each other.

Please visit my website jpfarr.com for supportive videos and other resources.

Again, thank you for taking the time and sharing your facilitation skills with others on the urgency of awareness!

APPENDIX

IDENTITY SOURCES

" The positive associations with right-handedness and the negative associations with left-handedness stretch to the words' origins. The Latin word for left, sinistra, also is the word for unlucky and is the root of the word sinister in English. Dexter, the root word for "right" in Latin, is the root of the English word dexterity, which means "the ability to use your hands skillfully."
Etymology of dexterity and sinister. *Merriam-Webster's Advanced Learner's English Dictionary.* Springfield, MA: Merriam-Webster, 2008.

Throughout history, left-handedness has been associated with being clumsy, awkward, and evil. The Old English word for left is lyft, which means weak or worthless. As recently as the 1970s, teachers often forced left-handed students to write with their right hands, sometimes using corporal punishment to enforce the norm.
Hardyck, Curtis, and Lewis F. Petrinovich. "Left-handedness." *Psychological Bulletin* 84, no. 3 (1977): 385-404. doi:10.1037/0033-2909.84.3.385.

Machinery, scissors, school desks, and even spiral-bound notebooks are formatted for the estimated 90 percent of the population that is right-handed. Using heavy machinery made for right-handed people can increase safety risks for left-handed people
Coren, Stanley. *The Left-hander Syndrome*: The Causes and Consequences of Left-handedness. New York: Free Press, 1992.

After more than four decades of serving as the nation's economic majority, the American middle class is now matched in number by those in the economic tiers above and below it. In early 2015, 120.8 million adults were in middle-income households, compared with 121.3 million in lower- and upper-income households combined, a demographic shift that could signal a tipping point, according to a new Pew Research Center analysis of government data.
Pew Research Center Analysis of the Current Population Survey, Annual Social and Economic Supplements, 1971 and 2015.

2016 Poverty Guidelines for the 48 Contiguous States and the District of Columbia.
Department of Health and Human Services Document 2016-01450 at pp. 4036 -4037 (January 25, 2016). 2016 Poverty Guidelines for the 48 Contiguous States and the District of Columbia. Document Citation: 81 FR 4036. https://federalregister.gov/a/2016-01450
Zoning laws, federal investment in highways and su
bsidizing of the auto industry, federally guaranteed loans that boosted suburban housing construction and other federal, state, and local initiatives encouraged middle-income families to establish neighborhoods outside of urban centers and away from lower-income residents.

"Our modern image of the middle class comes from the post-World War II era. The 1944 GI Bill provided returning veterans with money for college, businesses and home mortgages. Suddenly, millions of servicemen were able to afford homes of their own for the first time. As a result, residential construction jumped from 114,000 new homes in 1944 to 1.7 million in 1950."
Suddath, Claire. "A Brief History of the Middle Class." Time, Feb. 27, 2009. http://content.time.com/time/nation/article/0,8599,1882147,00.html.

IDENTITY   SOURCES

"After World War II, the Federal Housing Administration facilitated cheap loans to stimulate a boom in suburban housing construction. Called bedroom communities, some suburbs were designed for family and leisure time only, with work taking place in the city. The government subsidized the American auto industry by encouraging people to move to the suburbs and buy cars...The growth of the suburbs largely created the role of the middle class by giving them added chores in larger houses with lawns and gardens."

Boundless. Boundless U.S. History. The Growth of Suburbs. n.p., 2016. https://www.boundless.com/u-s-history/textbooks/boundless-u-s-his-tory-textbook/politics-and-culture-of-abundance-1943-1960-28/cul-ture-of-abundance-215/the-growth-of-suburbs-1196-5264/.

"New Deal labor law provided legal protections that enabled workers to organize unions and to negotiate for higher wages and benefits and for safe working conditions. New Deal legislation put a floor under labor stan-dards, establishing a minimum wage and overtime protections that lifted the incomes of workers across the wage spectrum. The New Deal's social insurance programs, including Social Security, unemployment insurance, government guarantees for home mortgages, and financial support for poor families with children, worked hand in hand with labor organizing and wage standards to build a broad middle class."

Kirsch, Richard. "The New Deal Launched Unions as Key to Building Mid-dle Class - Roosevelt Institute." Next New Deal: The Blog of the Roosevelt Institute. March 25, 2014. Accessed July 11, 2016. http://rooseveltinstitute. org/new-deal-launched-unions-as-key-building-middle-class.

"As the nation grapples with the growing gap between rich and poor and an economy increasingly reliant on formal education, public policies should address housing market regulations that prohibit all but the very affluent from enrolling their children in high-scoring public schools in order to pro-mote individual social mobility and broader economic security."

Rothwell, Jonathan. "Housing Costs, Zoning, and Access to High-Scoring Schools." Brookings Institute Metropolitan Housing Program. April 2012. http://www.brookings.edu/~/media/research/files/papers/2012/4/19%20 school%20inequality%20rothwell/0419_school_inequality_rothwell.pdf.

"What challenges do people with intersex conditions and their families face? Intersex conditions...whether discovered at birth or later in life, can be very challenging for affected persons and their families. Medical infor-mation about intersex conditions and their implications are not always easy to understand. Persons with intersex conditions and their families may also experience feelings of shame, isolation, anger, or depression."

Schneider, Margaret, Walter O. Bockting, Randall D. Ehrbar, Anne A. Lawrence, Atherine L. Rachlin, and Kenneth J. Zucker. Answers to Your Questions About Individuals with Intersex Conditions. Washington, DC: American Psychological Association, 2006. Produced by the APA Office of Public and Member Communications.

When women began to take more traditionally male jobs during World War II, the federal government asked employers to equalize pay for women and men. Employers refused, and as recently as the early 1960s, employers posted job listings categorized by gender. Even if the jobs were identical, employers would often pay women less than men.

Kopelov, Connie. "Pay Equity Information." History of the Struggle for Fair Pay. National Committee on Pay Equity. August 1999. Accessed July 11, 2016. http://pay-equity.org/info-history.html.

IDENTITY   SOURCES

Title VII of the 1964 Civil Rights Act prohibited gender discrimination in the workplace, and the 1963 Equal Pay Act prohibited pay discrimination on the basis of gender. In 2012, however, the most recent year for which federal data was available, women who worked full time earned 81 percent of what full-time male workers earned.
"Highlights of Women's Earnings in 2012." Report 1045. U.S. Bureau of Labor Statistics. October 2013. http://www.bls.gov/cps/cpswom2012.pdf.

At 474 of the 500 companies on the 2014 Fortune 500 list, men are the CEOs. Women hold 5.2 percent of the Fortune 500 CEO spots and just 5.4 percent of Fortune 1000 CEO jobs.
"Women CEOs of the S&P 500." Catalyst. July 1, 2016. http://catalyst.org/knowledge/women-ceos-fortune-1000.

Women make up more than 50 percent of the US population but just 18 percent of the members of the 114th Congress.
"New Members of the 114th Congress." National Journal. Dec. 17, 2014. http://www.nationaljournal.com/almanac/114th-congress-new-members.
"Sex Discrimination in the American Workplace: Still a Fact of Life." National Women's Law Center. June 30, 2000. http://www.nwlc.org/resource/sex-discrimination-american-workplace-still-fact-life.

Women hold 57 percent of jobs nationwide but only 25 percent in computing occupations, where the pay is far higher than in other industries.
Khanna, Derek. "We Need More Women in Tech: The Data Prove It," The Atlantic. Oct. 29, 2013. http://www.theatlantic.com/technology/archive/2013/10/we-need-more-women-in-tech-the-data-prove-it/280964/.

Online students are more likely to give professors higher evaluations if they think the instructors are male.
MacNell, Lillian and Matt Shipman. "What's in a Name: Exposing Gender Bias in Student Ratings of Teaching." Innovative Higher Education. Dec. 9, 2014. https://news.ncsu.edu/2014/12/macnell-gender-2014/.

Differently abled adults and children had no legal protection from discrimination prior to the passage of the Rehabilitation Act of 1973 and the Education for All Handicapped Children Act of 1975. Despite those laws, differently abled people were not fully protected until the passage of the 1990 Individuals with Disabilities Education Act (IDEA) and the 1990 Americans with Disabilities Act.
"A Brief History of the Disability Rights Movement." Anti-Defamation League. Accessed Dec. 29, 2014. http://archive.adl.org/education/curriculum_connections/fall_2005/fall_2005_lesson5_history.html.

"Discrimination based on disability is often caused by discomfort and pity or misguided compassion that materializes as paternalistic and patronizing behavior. For example, a restaurant owner who fails to provide a wheelchair ramp to the restaurant's entrance is more likely to be guilty of failing to consider the needs of patrons than of expressing a specific dislike of wheelchair users."
"Disability Discrimination." West's Encyclopedia of American Law. Accessed Dec. 29, 2014. http://www.encyclopedia.com/doc/1G2-3437701412.html.

Differently abled people are more likely to be poor than able-bodied people. "Twice as many Americans with disabilities live in poverty compared to those without disabilities. Over 28 percent of non-institutionalized adults

IDENTITY   SOURCES

aged 21–64 with a disability in the United States live in poverty compared to 12.4 percent of those without a disability; greater than the rate for any other demographic category including African-Americans, Hispanics, or female-headed households."
Committee on Health, Education, Labor & Pensions. "Fulfilling the Promise: Overcoming Persistent Barriers to Economic Self-Sufficiency for People with Disabilities." U.S. Senate, Majority Committee Staff Report. Sept. 18, 2014. http://www.help.senate.gov/imo/media/doc/HELP%20Committee%20 Disability%20and%20Poverty%20Report.pdf.

Eighty percent of differently abled people want to work, according to a 2014 study, yet are far more likely to be unemployed. "Of the 20 million adults with disabilities of working age, 80 percent want to work, the report says. But fewer than one-third are in the workforce, compared with 77 percent of Americans who don't have disabilities."
Resmovits, Joy. "Americans With Disabilities Are More Likely To Be Poor, Report Finds." Huffington Post. Sept. 18, 2014. http://www.huffingtonpost. com/2014/09/18/americans-with-disabiliti_n_5839476.html.

Despite exposure to extensive news coverage of disabled athletes, a study showed that unconscious bias against the disabled was higher in London after the 2012 Paralympics Games than before the games.
"Unconscious Bias against Disabled People is higher now than before the Paralympics." Employers Network for Equality and Inclusion. July 7, 2014. http://www.enei.org.uk/news.php/691/unconscious-bias-against-disabled-people-is-higher-now-than-before-the-paralympics.

One out of five Americans reports having a mental illness or disorder at some point in his or her life. The 1990 Americans with Disabilities Act prohibited discrimination against people with differently abled minds, but nearly ten years after its passage, the US Surgeon General still found that stigma against people with differently abled minds persisted.
"Stigma assumes many forms, both subtle and overt. It appears as prejudice and discrimination, fear, distrust, and stereotyping. It prompts many people to avoid working, socializing, and living with people who have a mental disorder. Stigma impedes people from seeking help for fear the confidentiality of their diagnosis or treatment will be breached."
"Facts about Stigma and Mental Illness in Diverse Communities, National Alliance for the Mentally Ill." U.S. Surgeon General's Report on Mental Health: 1999. Accessed Dec. 29, 2014. http://profiles.nlm.nih.gov/ps/access/NNBBHS.pdf.

In 2014, the federal government began to determinedly enforce a 1999 US Supreme Court ruling [Olmstead v. L. C. 527 U.S. 581 (1999)] that prohibits states from segregating "people with serious mental illnesses in psychiatric institutions if they were willing and able to live more independently in the community."

"One of those states was North Carolina, which agreed in a 2012 settlement with the Justice Department to move at least 3,000 people with serious mental illnesses into independent living by 2020, as long as they wanted to move."
McCrummen, Stephanie. "In Transition to Independent Living, the 'Dignity of Risk' for the Mentally Ill." The Washington Post. Dec. 27, 2014. http://www.washingtonpost.com/national/in-transition-to-independent-living-the-dignity-of-risk-for-the-mentally-ill/2014/12/27/dece-c1ee-8ad6-11e4-9e8d-0c687bc18da4_story.html.

IDENTITY   SOURCES

Despite federal legislation that prohibits discrimination against people with mental illness, many people with differently abled minds chose to hide their condition from employers and coworkers.

"The most frustrating part of my situation is that I can count on one hand the number of people who know about my mental illness. The stigma that surrounds mental health is suffocating, and I don't feel comfortable talking about it with most of my friends and family, and certainly not my boss or colleagues."
Laymon, CJ. "Why I Keep My Bipolar Disorder Secret at Work." Atlantic. Aug. 22, 2013. http://www.theatlantic.com/health/archive/2013/08/why-i-keep-my-bipolar-disorder-secret-at-work/278931/.

Race and color is highly subjective. Nonetheless, people have attempted to sort populations based on heritage and physical characteristics, even when it is scientifically invalid. These labels where to ensure that some people (ie people of color) would not be allowed the same access to the societal system. Although the Fifteenth Amendment of 1870 gave blacks the right to vote, Southern states devised all sorts of tests and devices to keep African Americans from the polls, forcing the federal government to pass the 1965 Voting Rights Act.

"Congress determined that the existing federal anti-discrimination laws were not sufficient to overcome the resistance by state officials to enforcement of the 15th Amendment. The legislative hearings showed that the Department of Justice's efforts to eliminate discriminatory election practices by litigation on a case-by-case basis had been unsuccessful in opening up the registration process; as soon as one discriminatory practice or procedure was proven to be unconstitutional and enjoined, a new one would be substituted in its place and litigation would have to commence anew."

"President Johnson signed the resulting legislation into law on August 6, 1965. Section 2 of the Act, which closely followed the language of the 15th amendment, applied a nationwide prohibition against the denial or abridgment of the right to vote on the literacy tests on a nationwide basis."
The Voting Rights Act of 1965. U.S. Department of Justice. Accessed Dec. 30, 2014. http://www.justice.gov/crt/about/vot/intro/intro_b.php.

"Despite Supreme Court decisions, including Shelley v. Kraemer (1948) and Jones v. Mayer Co. (decided in June 1968), barring the exclusion of African Americans or other minorities from certain sections of cities, race-based housing patterns were still in force by the late 1960s, and those who challenged them often met with resistance, hostility and even violence."
"Fair Housing Act of 1968," History.com. Accessed Dec. 29, 2014. http://www.history.com/topics/black-history/fair-housing-act.

As recently as 2013, research found that racial and ethnic minorities faced significant housing discrimination. "A new study has found that blacks, Latinos, and Asians looking for homes were shown fewer housing options than whites who were equally qualified. And fewer options meant higher housing costs."
Demby, Gene. "For People of Color, a Housing Market Partially Hidden From View." NPR.com. June 17, 2013.
http://www.npr.org/blogs/codeswitch/2013/06/17/192730233/for-people-of-color-a-housing-market-partially-hidden-from-view

IDENTITY   SOURCES

"US's top-paid executives in 2012 represent technology, coffee, and sporting goods companies – and all are white and male."
Rushe, Dominic. "The 10 highest-paid CEOs in America are all white men."
Guardian. Oct. 22, 2013. http://www.theguardian.com/business/2013/
oct/22/best-paid-chief-executives-america.

"A white [sounding] name yields as many or more callbacks as an additional eight years of experience," researchers found. Job applicants with
white-sounding names (Emily and Greg) were 50 percent more likely to get
a call for an interview than applications with African American [sounding]
names (Lakisha and Jamal).
"Employers' Replies to Racial Names." National Bureau of Economic Research. Accessed Jan. 1, 2015. http://www.nber.org/digest/sep03/w9873.
html.

In a short video, author and educator Joy DeGruy talks about a trip to the
grocery store and how her sister-in-law stood up to systemic inequity.
"A Trip to the Grocery Store." Cracking the Codes: The System of Racial
Inequity. Accessed Jan. 1, 2015. https://www.youtube.com/watch?v=W-
f9QBnPK6Yg.

The black/white wealth gap is the highest it's been since 1989 and has
worsened since the end of the Great Recession in 2009. Research indicates that the worsening gap is due to decreases in income in minority
households that outpaced white households. …

Financial assets, such as stocks, have recovered in value more quickly
than housing since the recession ended. White households are much more
likely than minority households to own stocks directly or indirectly through
retirement accounts. Thus, they were in better position to benefit from the
recovery in financial markets....
The current gap between blacks and whites has reached its highest point
since 1989, when whites had 17 times the wealth of black households. The
current white-to-Hispanic wealth ratio has reached a level not seen since
2001."

Kochhar, Rakesh and Richard Fry. "Wealth Inequality has widened along
racial, ethnic lines since the end of the Great Recession." Pew Research
Center. December 2014. http://www.pewresearch.org/fact-tank/2014/12/12/
racial-wealth-gaps-great-recession/.

"Because of racist policies like redlining, midcentury black families were
regularly cut off from the housing market, forced into predatory lending
arrangements when they did buy, and settled in neighborhoods that were
eventually decimated by white flight and urban decay. For the American
middle class, homeownership is wealth, and without it, blacks weren't able
to save and build assets to pass on to the next generation. In more recent
years, subprime lenders specifically targeted minority communities with the
risky loans that later led to the foreclosure crisis. The story is complicated.
But the upshot is simple: When it comes to finances, the U.S. has left the
typical black household with just about nothing."

Weissmann, Jordan. "The Wealth Gap Between Blacks and Whites Is Even
More Enormous (and Shameful) Than You Think." Slate.com. Dec. 15,
2014. http://www.slate.com/blogs/moneybox/2014/12/15/the_black_white_
wealth_gap_it_s_bigger_than_you_even_think.html.

IDENTITY   SOURCES

As recently as 1973, the American Psychiatric Association included homosexuality as a mental disorder in the Diagnostic and Statistical Manual of Mental Disorders.
Sullivan, Gail. "Man sues doctor for listing homosexuality as 'chronic condition' in his medical records." Washington Post. Aug. 14, 2014. http://www.washingtonpost.com/news/morning-mix/wp/2014/08/14/man-sues-doctor-for-listing-homosexuality-as-chronic-condition-in-his-medical-records/.

Despite a 2003 US Supreme Court ruling outlawing sodomy laws, twelve states still have anti-sodomy laws on the books.
"12 States Still Ban Sodomy a Decade after Court Ruling." USA Today. April 21, 2014. http://www.usatoday.com/story/news/nation/2014/04/21/12-states-ban-sodomy-a-decade-after-court-ruling/7981025/.

One-fifth of LGBT workers say they have experienced workplace discrimination because of their sexual orientation.
Brown, Anna. "As Congress considers action again, 21% of LGBT adults say they faced workplace discrimination." Pew Research Center. Nov. 4, 2013. http://www.pewresearch.org/fact-tank/2013/11/04/as-congress-considers-action-again-21-of-lgbt-adults-say-they-faced-workplace-discrimination/.

In 2011, the US House of Representatives passed a resolution reasserting that "In God We Trust" is the national motto. For years, atheists and secularists have fought to have references to a Christian deity removed from US currency.
"'In God We Trust' Reaffirmed As National Motto By House Of Representatives." Huffington Post. Jan. 2, 2012. http://www.huffingtonpost.com/2011/11/02/house-in-god-we-trust_n_1071180.html.

"The motto in god we trust was placed on United States coins largely because of the increased religious sentiment existing during the Civil War."
"History of 'In God We Trust.'" U.S. Department of the Treasury. Accessed Dec. 29, 2014. http://www.treasury.gov/about/education/Pages/in-god-we-trust.aspx.

In 2014, the US Supreme Court ruled that elected bodies can open meetings with prayer, even if it favors a particular religion.

"A New York town's practice of opening its government meetings with a prayer does not violate the constitutional separation of church and state, a sharply divided Supreme Court ruled Monday."
Somers, Meredith. "Divided Supreme Court OKs prayer before public meetings." Washington Times. May 5, 2014. http://www.washingtontimes.com/news/2014/may/5/divided-court-oks-prayer-public-meetings/?page=all.

A record number of Muslims reported workplace discrimination in 2009.
Greenhouse, Steven. "Muslims Report Rising Discrimination at Work." New York Times. Sept. 23, 2010. http://www.nytimes.com/2010/09/24/business/24muslim.html?pagewanted=all.

According to a 2014 survey, Christians, Jews, and Catholics are viewed warmly by Americans, but Muslims and atheists are viewed coldly.
"How Americans Feel About Religious Groups: Jews, Catholics & Evangelicals Rated Warmly, Atheists and Muslims More Coldly." Pew Research Center. July 16, 2014. http://www.pewforum.org/2014/07/16/how-americans-feel-about-religious-groups/.

IDENTITY   SOURCES

While the United States does not have an official national language, thirty-one states have "some sort of official English law," according to the English-only advocacy group US English. "Declaring English the official language means that official government business at all levels must be conducted solely in English."
"What Is Official English?" U.S. English. Accessed Dec. 29, 2014. http://www.us-english.org/view/9.

"English-only" movements are sometimes fueled by anti-immigrant sentiments; such sentiments helped pass a 1998 referendum in California that limited bilingual education. "Rejecting bilingual education was a way to 'send a message' that, in the United States, English and only English is appropriate for use in the public square."
Crawford, James. "A nation divided by one language." Guardian. March 7, 2001. http://www.theguardian.com/theguardian/2001/mar/08/guardianweek-ly.guardianweekly11.

The labels "formal English" and "casual English" often serve as stand-ins for value judgments placed on the speakers. "The myths of standard and substandard English do just that, permitting those in power to label others inferior on the basis of their 'broken' language."
Fox, Margalit. "The Way We Live Now: 9-12-99: On Language; Dialects." New York Times. Sept. 12, 1999. http://www.nytimes.com/1999/09/12/magazine/the-way-we-live-now-9-12-99-on-language-dialects.html?n=Top/Reference/Times%20Topics/People/F/Fox,%20Margalit.

"The English-only movement can have negative consequences on psychosocial development, intergroup relations, academic achievement, and psychometric and health-service delivery systems for many American citizens and residents who are not proficient in English."
"The English-Only Movement: Myths, Reality, and Implications for Psychol-ogy," American Psychological Association, Panel of Experts on English-On-ly Legislation. Accessed Dec. 29, 2014. http://www.apa.org/pi/oema/resources/english-only.aspx.

"The 'English Only' law has the effect, however, of marginalizing and de-meaning non-native English speakers, decreases the likelihood of creating and maintaining multilingual programs, and gives us all the false impres-sion that languages beside English are unimportant to learn, even though most other countries on the planet promote multilingualism."
Blumenfeld, Warren J. "'English Only' Laws Divide and Demean." Huffing-ton Post. Nov. 16, 2012. http://www.huffingtonpost.com/warren-j-blumen-feld/english-only-laws-divide-_b_2141330.html.

The 1944 Servicemen's Readjustment Act, better known as the GI Bill, provided World War II veterans the opportunity to attend college and shifted the focus of post-secondary training away from vocational schools to four-year colleges and universities. Today, a college degree is seen as a prerequisite for almost all middle-class careers.

"Studies conducted at the time estimated that 1,400,000 'man-years' of undergraduate training had been lost because of the war, due to the large number of young men unable to attend school. Moreover, the decade of economic depression that preceded the war created a generation of work-ers who were not only lacking in education but also in any meaningful work experience. Thus, Title II would 'aid in replenishing the nation's human capital' which had been ravaged by years of depression and war."

IDENTITY   SOURCES

Batten, Dayne D. "The G.I. Bill, Higher Education and American Society." Grove City College Journal of Law & Public Policy. Spring 2011. http://www2.gcc.edu/orgs/gclawjournal/articles/spring%202011/gi%20bill.pdf.

"Jobs that once required less than a bachelor's degree—administrative assistants, computer support specialists and food service managers, for example—are now often marketed as positions that require a college education. The shift in workforce demands comes in part from some jobs that have changed over time—perhaps in requiring more sophisticated skills or credentials—and partly because employers see a bachelor's degree as a recruitment tool for weeding out undesirable candidates."

Bidwell, Allie. "How 'Upcredentialing' May Close the Middle-Class Path." U.S. News and World Report. Sept. 9, 2014. http://www.usnews.com/news/articles/2014/09/09/report-employers-want-more-college-graduates-for-lower-level-jobs.

The profession of law enforcement has shifted from one that did not require post-secondary education to one that does. The reasoning was that "if law enforcement officers became more professional, then the unprofessional actions of law enforcement officers would be curtailed. This approach seemed reasonable; but the basis for the commissions' findings and recommendations was anecdotal stories and assumed correlations between education and improved police officer behavior."

Bostrom, Matthew D. "The Influence of Higher Education on Police Officer Work Habits." Police Chief Magazine. October 2005. http://www.police-chiefmagazine.org/magazine/index.cfm?fuseaction=display_arch&article_id=722&issue_id=102005#3.

"There are several advantages of being employed. Check out the 7 benefits of working for money.

1.Financial independence

The first and foremost advantage of being employed is the financial independence that you get. You earn the money, so you can spend it the way you want. No need to ask for pocket money or beg before friends to fund your needs.

2. Financial security

Since employment promises a salary at regular intervals, you feel financially secure. You can spend money according to your whims and fancies and yet, rest assured, you still have money in your pocket! Secondly, you can save money for yourself or for your family.

3. Medical benefit

In most companies, employees are allowed to opt for a medical insurance whose cost is beared by the company. Imagine, you need a huge sum of money for an emergency operation and you don't have to pay for it! Also, many get paid for the sick leaves that they avail of. Even if your company doesn't pay you a separate amount for your medical insurance, you can always save money for a crisis situation.

4. Talent put to use

When you work in the field you love, you get to put your talent to use. Say, graphics is your cup of tea. Pursuing a career as a graphic designer would not only make your work an enjoyable process but will also hone your talent.

5. Productive Use of Time

When you are employed at a place, you tend to make a productive use of your time. And, of course, you get money for it! It's definitely better than whiling away time at your home or your friends' place.

IDENTITY   SOURCES

6. Professional growth
When you are employed for a longer duration, you achieve professional growth. You can reach places in a matter of a few years. This also means you will earn more, save more and, of course, spend more.
7. Adds to your knowledge
When you are employed, you get to learn thousands of new things. If you change workplaces, you got to know new business ideas. Apart from that, you also get to know how different companies work. So, when you plan to quit your job and start your own business, you will be ready for the feat."

7 Advantages Of Being Employed. (2011, May 18). Retrieved from Mag For Women website: http://www.magforwomen.com/7-advantages-of-being-employed/#sq6uWGwrEgYME3c4.99

The federal government and society confer hundreds of benefits on married couples that do not extend to single adults.
"[M]ore than 1,000 laws provide overt legal or financial benefits to married couples. Marital privileging marginalizes the 50 percent of Americans who are single."
Arnold, Lisa and Campbell, Christina. "The High Price of Being Single in America." Atlantic. Jan. 14, 2013. http://www.theatlantic.com/sexes/archive/2013/01/the-high-price-of-being-single-in-america/267043/.
"Historically, governments have passed laws encouraging marriage and families in the hopes that doing so would decrease the likelihood that the state would need to care for abandoned children."
Kelly, Maura. "Singled Out: Are Unmarried People Discriminated Against?" Daily Beast. Feb. 6, 2012. http://www.thedailybeast.com/articles/2012/02/06/singled-out-are-america-s-unmarried-discriminated-against.html

Among the government benefits married couples receive are survivor's benefits from a pension plan, gift tax marital deduction, and estate tax marital deduction.
Ashford, Kate. "11 Things You Never Thought of When You Decided Not to Get Married." Forbes.com. Sept. 26, 2014. http://www.forbes.com/sites/kateashford/2014/09/26/deciding-not-to-get-married/.

A 2014 study found that 46 percent of respondents said society is better off when marriage and children are a priority.
Wang, Wendy and Kim Parker. "Record Share of Americans Have Never Married." Pew Research Center. Sept. 24, 2014. http://www.pewsocialtrends.org/2014/09/24/record-share-of-americans-have-never-married/.

The 1967 Age Discrimination in Employment Act was passed in after congressional findings established that "in the face of rising productivity and affluence, older workers find themselves disadvantaged in their efforts to retain employment, and especially to regain employment when displaced from jobs."

The act was designed to "promote employment of older persons based on their ability rather than age; to prohibit arbitrary age discrimination in employment; to help employers and workers find ways of meeting problems arising from the impact of age on employment."

Text of Age Discrimination in Employment Act of 1967. Equal Employment Opportunity Commission. Accessed Dec. 29, 2014.http://www.eeoc.gov/eeoc/history/35th/thelaw/adea67.html.

IDENTITY   SOURCES

The Age Discrimination in Employment Act followed New York surveys in the late 1950s that found "42 percent of firms had maximum age restrictions of 50 for new hires."
Neumark, David. "Age Discrimination Legislation in the United States." National Bureau of Economic Research. March 2001. http://www.nber.org/papers/w8152.pdf.

"Workers 50 and older are less likely than younger workers to lose their jobs, but they take longer to find work when they become unemployed, especially in the Great Recession."
Johnson, Richard W. and Janice S. Park. "Can Unemployed Older Workers Find Work?" Urban Institute. January 2011. http://www.urban.org/uploaded-pdf/412283-Unemployed-Older-Workers.pdf.

Older people are often assumed to be infirm and incapable of handling their own affairs, regardless of whether they have shown any diminished capacity.

"Store clerks, bank tellers, government workers, pharmacists, hairdressers, nurses, receptionists, and doctors alike ignore the older person and pay attention exclusively to the younger companion, regardless of who is the actual customer or patient. 'Older people are invisible in society after a certain point,' said Nancy Perry Graham, editor in chief of AARP The Magazine, the flagship publication of the advocacy group for people over age 50. 'It's one of the last remaining acceptable prejudices.'"
Hawthorne, Fran. "Talk to Me, Not to My Daughter." New York Times. May 9, 2012. http://www.nytimes.com/2012/05/10/business/retirementspecial/talking-past-older-people-to-their-younger-companions.html?pagewanted=all&_r=0.

Many unfounded stereotypes about older workers persist, including that older workers are less motivated, are more likely to have health problems that affect their ability to work, and are resistant to change.
Ng, Thomas W. H. and Daniel C. Feldman. "Stereotypes and the Older Worker." Personnel Psychology. November 2012. http://www.strategy-business.com/article/re00225?gko=70968.

The Twenty-Sixth Amendment, which lowered the voting age to eighteen, was passed in 1971, after years of debate following World War II and the Vietnam War.

"The long debate over lowering the voting age in America from 21 to 18 began during World War II and intensified during the Vietnam War, when young men denied the right to vote were being conscripted to fight for their country."
"The 26th Amendment." History.com. Last accessed Dec. 31, 2014. http://www.history.com/topics/the-26th-amendment.

Even though there is no scientific evidence establishing at what age children become capable of making adult decisions, eighteen has been considered the age of majority because it is also the age at which young people can vote.
Lai, Jennifer. "Old Enough to Vote, Old Enough to Smoke?" Slate.com. April 23, 2013. http://www.slate.com/articles/news_and_politics/explainer/2013/04/new_york_minimum_smoking_age_why_are_young_people_considered_adults_at_18.html.

IDENTITY

SOURCES

The federal government offers many tax benefits to parents with children under the age of eighteen.
"Eight Tax Benefits for Parents." IRS.gov. Feb. 11, 2013. http://www.irs.gov/uac/Newsroom/Eight-Tax-Benefits-for-Parents

Men and women tend to have very different workplace experiences after having children. Working fathers often receive what's called the "daddy bonus"—a growth in income as they considered more stable and because they are now supporting a family. Conversely, working mothers experience the "motherhood penalty"—because they couldn't possibly be fully committed to their career after becoming a mother, they are given less consideration for advancement and raises.

"One of the worst career moves a woman can make is to have children. Mothers are less likely to be hired for jobs, to be perceived as competent at work or to be paid as much as their male colleagues with the same qualifications. For men, meanwhile, having a child is good for their careers. They are more likely to be hired than childless men, and tend to be paid more after they have children. These differences persist even after controlling for factors like the hours people work, the types of jobs they choose and the salaries of their spouses."
Miller, Claire Cain. "The Motherhood Penalty vs. the Fatherhood Bonus: A Child Helps Your Career, if You're a Man." New York Times. Sept. 6, 2014. http://www.nytimes.com/2014/09/07/upshot/a-child-helps-your-career-if-youre-a-man.html?_r=0

Birth certificates, marriage licenses, and many government documents only provide for two gender options: male or female.
"For transgender people, identification documents and other official records frequently function as something akin to a scarlet letter, with the 'F' or 'M' designation contradicting the holder's appearance and social identity and outing him or her as transgender. State and federal policies in the United States today make it impossible for many transgender people to update these documents to reflect their lived gender. These restrictive policies create not only an enormous indignity but a significant barrier to economic and other opportunities and at times even compromise personal safety."
Tobin, Harper Jean. "Fair and Accurate Identification for Transgender People." LGBTQ Policy Journal at the Harvard Kennedy School. 2011 Edition. http://isites.harvard.edu/icb/icb.do?keyword=k78405&pageid=icb.page414493.

Transgender people were four times as likely to have a household income under $10,000, and 41 percent reported attempting suicide, compared to 1.6 percent of the general population.

"Ninety percent (90%) of [transgender people] surveyed reported experiencing harassment, mistreatment or discrimination on the job or took actions like hiding who they are to avoid it."
Grant, Jaime M., Lisa A. Mottet, Justin Tanis, Jack Harrison, Jody L. Herman, and Mara Keisling. Injustice at Every Turn: A Report of the National Transgender Discrimination Survey. Washington: National Center for Transgender Equality and National Gay and Lesbian Task Force. 2011. Accessed Dec. 29, 2014. http://www.transequality.org/Resources/ntds_full.pdf.
"The D.C. Council is preparing to pass legislation that would make it easier for transgender people to obtain new birth certificates reflecting their change in sexual identity. ...The transgender community of about 500 people in D.C. faces tens of thousands of dollars in sex change operations and currently must advertise name changes in local publications for three

111

weeks."

Sherwood, Tom. "D.C. Council Moves Toward New Birth Certificates for Transgender People." NBC4 Washington. June 6, 2013. http://www.nbcwashington.com/blogs/first-read-dmv/DC-Council-Moves-Toward-New-Birth-Certificates-for-Transgender-People-210487051.html.

Across the country, schools and universities are taking steps to recognize and make accommodations for transgender individuals.

"Blake's Upper School will open 'All Genders Welcome' bathrooms on the main floors in January, becoming one of the first Minnesota schools to offer gender neutral bathrooms for students. Avalon, a charter school in St. Paul, is on the verge of opening a similar restroom. These schools are placing Minnesota among a growing list of states taking steps to ensure that transgender and gender nonconforming students feel safe and comfortable in school, whether that's using the restroom or getting dressed in a locker room. Many colleges and universities already have gender-neutral bathrooms and other public facilities, and now they are being opened in a growing number of high schools."

McGuire, Kim. "New school bathrooms seek to ensure that all genders feel safe and welcome." Minneapolis Star-Tribune. Dec. 25, 2014. http://strib.mn/1EmZt1L

"Undocumented immigrants are often taken advantage of by the people they work for. Employers might feel free to pay low wages and ignore dangerous conditions, because the workers have no legal way of complaining. If they go to the authorities, they risk being arrested themselves and deported. If they complain or make trouble in other ways, the bosses can call immigration and have them taken away. Landlords can do this too, forcing people to live in terrible conditions because they have no way to complain or fight back."
"Immigration: Living Undocumented." PBS Kids, accessed July 11, 2016. http://pbskids.org/itsmylife/family/immigration/article5.html.

"Based on a recent review of the literature, Caplan (2007) identified three major types of stressors among Latino immigrants: instrumental/environmental, social/interpersonal, and societal. Instrumental/environmental stressors include challenges related to obtaining the goods and services needed for one's day-today existence, such as employment, access to health care, and language abilities. Social and interpersonal stressors refer to challenges related to the reestablishment of sources of family and social support, changing gender roles and family, and intergenerational conflicts. Societal stressors capture discrimination and difficulties associated with undocumented status, including fear of deportation. Immigrants are likely to experience acculturative stress to the extent to which they experience these stressors and appraise them as threatening their wellbeing and taxing their coping resources."
Arbona C, Olvera N, Rodriguez N, Hagan J, Linares A, Wiesner M. Acculturative Stress Among Documented and Undocumented Latino Immigrants in the United States. Hispanic Journal of Behavioral Sciences. 2010;32(3):362-384. doi:10.1177/0739986310373210. http://www.ncbi.nlm.nih.gov/pmc/articles/PMC4254683/

"There are believed to be 11 million undocumented immigrants in the United States. We're not always who you think we are. Some pick your strawberries or care for your children. Some are in high school or college. And

IDENTITY   SOURCES

some, it turns out, write news articles you might read. I grew up here. This is my home. Yet even though I think of myself as an American and consider America my country, my country doesn't think of me as one of its own."
Jose Antonio Vargas. "My Life as an Undocumented Immigrant.," The New York Times, June 22, 2011, http://nyti.ms/1AkVM5y.

When Affirmative Action Was White, by Ian Katznelson (book) surveys the multiple stages in US history when non-European Americans were denied access. Discussion include legislation including, the New Deal, Segregationists positioning of National Labor Relations Act (1935) and the Fair Labor Standards Act (1938). Also included in the discourse are the implications of the Taft-Hartley Act (1944) and GI Bill. The analysis studies how key programs and legislation created and perpetuated discriminatory practices.
Katznelson, I. (2005). When affirmative action was white: An untold history of racial inequality in twentieth-century America. New York: W.W. Norton.

"To this general European heritage, the English added their common law and their prudent, prescriptive politics; and the English experience became directly part of the American social order. The founders of the American Republic, especially the lawyers and colonial representatives among them, took for granted this English pattern of politics, only modifying it slightly to suit the new nation."
Today, C. (1960, January 4). The Common Heritage of America and Europe. Retrieved August 13, 2010, from The Russell Kirk Center website: https://kirkcenter.org/history/the-common-heritage-of-america-and-europe/

"One in four Americans has a criminal record, as NPR's Carrie Johnson has reported. Those records can include arrests that never led to convictions, as well as convictions for a wide range of crimes — from petty to serious — that may have happened decades ago.
A record can make it hard to find a job — or a home. Many private landlords and public housing projects have policies against renting to people with criminal records."
Domonoske, C. (2016, April 4). Denying Housing Over Criminal Record May Be Discrimination, Feds Say. Retrieved from https://www.npr.org/sections/thetwo-way/2016/04/04/472878724/denying-housing-over-criminal-record-may-be-discrimination-feds-say.

Millions of Americans are excluded from our democratic process on the basis of criminal disenfranchisement laws. These laws strip voting rights from people with past criminal convictions — and they vary widely between states. Kentucky and Iowa impose lifetime disenfranchisement for all people with felony convictions — unless the government grants an individual pardon. And they are only 2 of the 32 states that bar community members from voting, simply on the basis of convictions in their past. Navigating this patchwork of state laws can be exceedingly difficult, especially because election officials often misunderstand their own states' laws.
Project, The Right to Vote. *"Criminal Disenfranchisement Laws Across the United States: Brennan Center for Justice."* Criminal Disenfranchisement Laws Across the United States | Brennan Center for Justice, www.brennancenter.org/criminal-disenfranchisement-laws-across-united-states.

NOTES

1. *"The Servicemen's Readjustment Act of 1944* provided for education and training, home, farm, and business loan guarantees, and unemployment pay for veterans."
"History and Timeline," U.S. Department of Veterans Affairs, www. benefits.va.gov/gibill/history.asp. (225D, n.d.)

2. *"The GI Bill made white flight, the mass exodus of whites from urban areas to the suburbs, a possibility. Fee policies contributed to the expanding racial wealth gap during the twentieth century by facilitating white wealth accumulation through access to home ownership, and inhibiting black wealth accumulation."*
Kathleen Fitzgerald, *Recognizing Race and Ethnicity: Power, Privilege, and Inequality.* New Orleans: Westview Press, Loyola University (2014). (Fitzgerald, 2014)

3. *"Let me make one principle of this administration abundantly clear: All of these increased opportunities—in employment, in education, in housing, and in every field—must be open to Americans of every color. As far as the writ of federal law will run, we must abolish not some, but all racial discrimination. For this is not merely an economic issue, or a social, political, or international issue. It is a moral issue, and it must be met by the passage this session of the bill now pending in the House."*
President Lyndon B. Johnson, State of the Union Address. January 8, 1964, Washington, DC. (W. Johnson, 1953)

4. "Considering women themselves were once property, we've come a long way: most women can now walk into a bank and open an account, sign up for a credit card, or take out a loan. As recently as the 1970s, credit cards were issued only with a husband's signature; it took the Equal Credit Opportunity Act of 1974 to force companies to make cards available to women." Covert, Bryce.

114

"The Nation: Financial Reform Could Hurt Women," National Public Radio, April 27, 2011. Retrieved January 11, 2016. http://n.pr/frvkEC (Covert, 2011)

BIBLIOGRAPHY

7 Advantages Of Being Employed. (2011, May 18). Retrieved from Mag For Women website: http://www.magforwomen.com/7-advantages-of-being-employed/#sq6uWGwrEgYME3c4.99

225D. (n.d.). History and Timeline–Education and Training. Retrieved from Va.gov website: https://benefits.va.gov/gibill/history.asp

Anim van Wyk. (2014, September 15). Do 40 000 whites own 80% of South Africa? Retrieved from The M&G Online website: https://mg.co.za/article/2014-09-15-do-40-000-whites-own-80-of-south-africa/

Babcock, L., & Laschever, S. (2007). *Women Don't Ask: the High Cost of Avoiding Negotiation and Positive Strategies for Change*. New York: Bantam Books.

Batalova, J. (2018, August 22). European Immigrants in the United States. Retrieved from migrationpolicy.org website: https://www.migrationpolicy.org/article/european-immigrants-united-states

Bernstein, E. (2012, July 24). Divorce's Guide to Marriage: The Five Lessons Divorced People Learn About Marriage. Retrieved October 6, 2016, from WSJ website: https://www.wsj.com/articles/SB10000872396390444025204577544951717564114

Bussey, J. (2014, October 10). Gender Wage Gap Reflects the 'Ask' Gap. Retrieved February 11, 2016, from WSJ website: https://www.wsj.com/articles/gender-wage-gap-reflects-the-ask-gap-1412980899

Cohen, M. (2012, October 30). South Africa's Racial Income Inequality Persists, Census Shows. Retrieved from Bloomberg.com website: https://www.bloomberg.com/news/articles/2012-10-30/south-africa-s-racial-income-inequality-persists-census-shows

Communication Tips for Parents and Teens. (n.d.). Retrieved September 24, 2015, from University of Wisconsin website: http://www.dce.k12.wi.us/pdfs/CommunicationTipsForParentsAndTeens.pdf

Covert, B. (2011, April 27). *The Nation: Financial Reform Could Hurt Women*. Retrieved from http://n.pr/frvkEC

Cunningham, B. (2007, December 30). Digital Native or Digital Immigrant, Which Language Do You Speak? Retrieved from Ksu.edu website: https://nacada.ksu.edu/Resources/Academic-Advising-Today/View-Articles/Digital-Native-or-Digital-Immigrant-Which-Language-Do-You-Speak.aspx

Definition of Left-Handed by Lexico. (n.d.). Retrieved from Lexico Dictionaries | English website: http://www.oxforddictionaries.com/us/definition/american_english/left-handed

Delgado, R., & Stefancic, J. (1997). *Critical white studies : looking behind the mirror.* Philadelphia: Temple University Press.

DeSilver, D. (2013, December 6). Chart of the Week: How South Africa changed, and didn't, over Mandela's lifetime. Retrieved from Pew Research Center website: https://www.pewresearch.org/fact-tank/2013/12/06/chart-of-the-week-how-south-africa-changed-and-didnt-over-mandelas-lifetime/

Dimitri, C., Effland, A., & Conklin, N. (2005). *The 20th Century Transformation of U.S. Agriculture and Farm Policy.* Retrieved from U.S. Department of Agriculture website: http://www.ers. usda.gov/media/259572/eib3_1_.pdf

Dörner, D. (1997). *The Logic of Failure: Recognizing and Avoiding Error in Complex Situations*. Boston: Addison-Wesley.

Dovidio, J. (n.d.). *Speaking of Psychology: Understanding Your Racial Biases, Episode 31* (A. Hamilton, Interviewer). Retrieved from https://www.apa.org/research/action/speaking-of-psychology/ understanding-biases

Eveleth, R. (2013, May 17). Two-Thirds of the World Still Hates Lefties. Retrieved from Smithsonian website: http://www.smithsonianmag.com/smart-news/ two-thirds-of-the-world-still-hates-lefties-64727388/?no-ist

Fields, S. (2004). The Fat of the Land: Do Agricultural Subsidies Foster Poor Health? *Environmental Health Perspectives*, 112(14). https:// doi.org/10.1289/ehp.112-a820

Fitzgerald, K. (2014). *RECOGNIZING RACE AND ETHNICITY, STUDENT ECONOMY EDITION: Power, Privilege, and Inequality*. New Orleans: Westview Press, Loyola University.

Good Service is Good Business: American Consumers Willing to Spend More With Companies That Get Service Right, According to American Express Survey. (2011, May 11). Retrieved from Businesswire.com website: https://www.businesswire.com/news/home/20110503005753/en/ Good-Service-Good-Business-American-Consumers-Spend

Grossman, S. (2012). Ellen DeGeneres Responds to Anti-Gay "One Million Moms" Group. Retrieved January 11, 2012, from TIME.com website: http://newsfeed.time.com/2012/02/08/ ellen-degeneres-addresses-anti-gay-one-million-moms-group

Haney, I. F. (2006). *White by law : the legal construction of race.* New York; London: University Press.

Johnson, L. (1964, January). *State of the Union Address, 1964.*

Johnson, W. (1953, January). The Fateful Process of Mr. A Talking to Mr. B. *Harvard Business Review, 49.*

Katznelson, I. (2005). *When Affirmative Action Was White: an Untold History of Racial Inequality in Twentieth-Century America.* New York: W.W. Norton.

Kon, Z. R., & Lackan, N. (2008). Ethnic Disparities in Access to Care in Post-Apartheid South Africa. *American Journal of Public Health, 98*(12), 2272–2277. https://doi.org/10.2105/ajph.2007.127829

Kushner, H. I. (2013). Why are there (almost) no left-handers in China? *Endeavour, 37*(2), 71–81. https://doi.org/10.1016/j. endeavour.2012.12.003

Lane, L. L. (n.d.). Reflective Listening. Retrieved January 12, 2016, from Jrank.org website: http://psychology.jrank.org/pages/536/ Reflective-Listening.html

Leibbrandt, M., Levinsohn, J., & McCrary, J. (2005). Incomes in South Africa since the Fall of Apartheid. *NBER Working Paper Series, No. 11384.* https://doi.org/10.3386/w11384

Leyden, K. M. (2003). Social Capital and the Built Environment: The Importance of Walkable Neighborhoods. *American Journal of Public Health, 93*(9), 1546–1551. https://doi.org/10.2105/ ajph.93.9.1546

Lucchesi, PhD, A., & Echo-Hawk, A. (2018). *Missing and Murdered Indigenous Women & Girls.* Retrieved from Urban Indian

Health Institute website: http://www.uihi.org/wp-content/
uploads/2018/11/Missing-and-Murdered-Indigenous-Women-
and-Girls-Report.pdf

Ludden, J. (2011, February 8). *Ask For a Raise? Most Women Hesitate*.
Retrieved from http://n.pr/h0bjtU

Mcintosh, P. (1988). *White Privilege and Male Privilege: a Personal
Account of Coming to See Correspondences through Work in
Women's Studies*. Wellesley, Ma: Wellesley College, Center For
Research On Women.

Mead, M. N. (2008). Urban Issues: The Sprawl of Food Deserts.
Environmental Health Perspectives, 116(8). https://doi.
org/10.1289/ehp.116-a335a

Morland, K., Wing, S., Diez Roux, A., & Poole, C. (2002). Neighborhood
characteristics associated with the location of food stores and food
service places. *American Journal of Preventive Medicine, 22*(1),
23–29. https://doi.org/10.1016/s0749-3797(01)00403-2

Population Clock. (n.d.). Retrieved from Census.gov website: http://
www.census.gov/popclock

Prensky, M. (2001). Digital Natives, Digital Immigrants Part 1. *On the
Horizon, 9*(5), 1–6. https://doi.org/10.1108/10748120110424816

RightNow Technologies. (2010, October 9). 2010 Customer
Experience Impact Report. Retrieved October 21, 2015,
from Slideshare.net website: http://www.slideshare.net/
RightNow/2010-customer-experience-impact

Sanchez-Burks, J., Lee, F., Choi, I., Nisbett, R., Zhao, S., & Koo, J.
(2003). Conversing across cultures: East-West communication

styles in work and nonwork contexts. *Journal of Personality and Social Psychology, 85*(2), 363–372. https://doi.org/10.1037/0022-3514.85.2.363

Schwatrtz, M. (2014). Being Heard: Breaking Through the Impasse. Retrieved October 6, 2016, from Psychology Today website: http://www.psychologytoday.com/blog/shift-mind/201401/being-heard-breaking-through-the-impasse

Simmons, R. (2014). *Success Through Stillness*. New York: Gotham Books.

Things to Do to Practice Better Commication. (n.d.). Retrieved September 25, 2015, from Relationships and Social Skills | Sutter Health website: http://www.pamf.org/teen/abc/buildingblocks/eightthings.html

Today, C. (1960, January 4). The Common Heritage of America and Europe. Retrieved August 13, 2010, from The Russell Kirk Center website: https://kirkcenter.org/history/the-common-heritage-of-america-and-europe/

Turner, S., & Bound, J. (2003). Closing the Gap or Widening the Divide: The Effects of the G.I. Bill and World War II on the Educational Outcomes of Black Americans. *The Journal of Economic History, 63*(1), 145–177.

United States Employment Rate. (2019, October 21). Retrieved from Tradingeconomics.com website: https://tradingeconomics.com/united-states/employment-rate